Social work

Library of Social Work

General Editor:
Noel Timms
Professor of Social Work Studies
University of Newcastle upon Tyne

Social work
Reform or revolution ?

Colin Pritchard

Director of Social Work Studies
University of Bath

and

Richard Taylor

Department of Adult Education
University of Leeds

Ex Libris
REGINALD VERNON

Routledge & Kegan Paul
London, Henley and Boston

*First published in 1978
by Routledge & Kegan Paul Ltd
39 Store Street,
London WC1E 7DD,
Broadway House,
Newtown Road,
Henley-on-Thames,
Oxon RG9 1EN and
9 Park Street,
Boston, Mass. 02108, USA
Set in 10/11 pt English
and printed in Great Britain by
The Lavenham Press Limited
Lavenham, Suffolk
© Colin Pritchard and Richard Taylor 1978
No part of this book may be reproduced in
any form without permission from the
publisher, except for the quotation of brief
passages in criticism*

British Library Cataloguing in Publication Data

Pritchard, Colin

*Social work. —(Library of social work; 0305-4381).
1. Social service—Great Britain—Political aspects
I. Title II. Taylor, Richard III. Series
361'.941   HV248*

*ISBN 0 7100 8882 5
ISBN 0 7100 8884 1 Pbk*

Contents

	Preface	vii
1	Social work and politics: an introduction	1
2	Tolerating uncertainty	7
3	Political culture of contemporary Britain (1): Conservatism	17
4	Political culture of contemporary Britain (2): social democracy	40
5	Political directions in social work	68
6	The problems of legitimation	88
7	Reform, revolution, or . . .?	110
	References	132
	Further reading	151
	Bibliography	153
	Index	159

Preface

The initial idea for this book evolved through discussions with students on the M.Sc. Mental Health Social Work course at Leeds University and we are grateful for their participation and insights in 1974, 1975 and 1976.

Several colleagues have offered valuable advice; particular thanks are due to Ray Jones and Mike Newman, both of whom read and commented upon substantial sections of the book.

We are grateful to Noel Timms, the editor of this series, for his initial encouragement and his continued support during the preparation of the book.

Our numerous intellectual debts will be obvious from the text.

Finally, thanks are due to Margaret Aykroyd, Gill Fieldhouse and Betty Sinclair who typed the initial drafts of the book.

For any inaccuracies and infelicities which remain, we are, of course, entirely responsible.

Colin Pritchard
Richard Taylor

Chapter one

Social work and politics: an introduction

The aim of this book is to examine contemporary British social work in its political context. Politics is fundamentally about power and power relationships in society. Bernard Crick has defined 'Politics' as 'the activity by which differing interests within a given unit of rule are conciliated by giving them a share in power in proportion to their importance to the welfare and the survival of the whole community'.[1] This definition is useful and unexceptionable but raises more questions than it solves: how for instance can the relative importance of different interests in the community be determined? The central political questions must thus be concerned with power: how *is* power distributed in society and how *ought* power to be distributed?

Some would argue strongly that political concerns of this type have no relevance to social work. (As Ray Lees says in the very first sentence of his book *Politics and Social Work*:[2] 'It may be the case that social workers are less interested in politics (or perhaps more disillusioned about them) than any other subject that could be discussed in social work literature.') We will be concerned with the position of social work within the social totality and will argue that social work necessarily has a relationship of continuous tension arising from the conflicting roles of maintaining the consensus (and acting as an agent of social control) and on occasions of being involved in conflict and confrontation situations against authority.

There are, within the professional ethos of British social work, four broadly held views of the function and essential nature of the institution that may apply not only to Britain but to any developed industrial society. To present a tetrarchy of views is to over-simplify a complex and subtle infrastructure but we would asset that these four divisions are identifiable and mark clear and important conceptual differences within the profession. These four views may be characterised as the moral-ethical; the psycho-pathological; the psycho-social and the radical-political.

The moral-ethical view sees social work as an apolitical activity—

an essentially individual and moral concern, a task consisting fundamentally of tidying-up societal loose ends and casualties, the concern being centred on the individual and the implicit assumption being that the problems, and hence the need for a social work function, are not peculiar to our society and would remain in any social system. Such an outlook sees social work as being concerned with those people who are socially inadequate and are unable to exist in a community at an acceptable level without both material and professional help. Thus social work of this orientation is predominantly concerned with the rescue and amelioration of individuals within this 'inadequate' category.[3] Although explicitly this is an apolitical view of the social work function there is a strong implicit ideological position that assumes much about the structure of society. Similarly, this position implies theories both of the aetiology of problematic situations and of the social forces that cause the 'inadequate' groups to come into being (and perpetuate their inadequacy).

This 'apolitical' view of social work has therefore much relevance to this political study and some time is spent examining the underlying political implications inherent in this view.

Alternatively social work can be seen, again apolitically, as a therapy exercise in which the social worker's role is to help people adjust to the dominant norms of society (thus by implication accepting at least in their professional roles the social structure as given). This psycho-pathological view of social work sees the need for 'treatment'—that is, some sort of intervention on behalf of society to another individual, but implies that the causal factors are exclusively within that person. Social work of this nature, like the moral-ethical type, has an essentially humane concern with personal amelioration added to a dimension of individualization. The overall aim is to liberate and maximize the individual's potential for complete, mature, personal expression. To facilitate this social work should, according to this view, support or bring about a personal adjustment that is compatible both with the individual's personality *and* with prevailing societal norms.[4] Again, this kind of help may well be needed in whatever type of society is established, for like the moral-ethical paradigm the psycho-pathological model sees the 'deviancy', the 'problem', as emanating from within the individual. Few modern social workers (even those of the Freudian and ego-dynamic schools) would in practice work in a purely uni-directional way, even though a fair proportion of clients may reasonably accurately be described within the psycho-pathological framework. This view, of course, has had a profound impact on social work attitudes[5] and has important political connotations which will require examination.

Social work and politics: an introduction

There are however, in our opinion, strong reasons for accepting that social work is a political activity and it is on the debates and conflicts within the parameters of these political conceptions that the main discussion in this book takes place.

The social work profession arose directly from changes in the social and economic structure and the consequent developments and shifts in the ideological outlook of opinion-forming groups within society.[6] The conceptual and the actual development of Welfare Statism in the twentieth century exemplifies more eloquently than abstract arguments the importance of both social and political structure and thought in the development of social work.

In this context an understanding of the historical development of British political culture is crucial. The social work profession has its roots in the unique social and political culture of nineteenth- and twentieth-century Britain and none of the conceptions of social work can be fully understood without an appreciation of the overall political and historical context. Chapters 3 and 4 are thus devoted to an account of the development of British political culture and the ways in which social work emerged from this background. Just as important as the fertile political ground out of which social work grew is the highly sensitive political area in which mainstream social work now operates. Whereas some groups in society, such as the police, have an overtly political function, in that their ultimate *raison d'être* is the support of the existing social and political system, and other groups such as extremist political organizations have an equally overt (oppositional) political role, social work is in a unique position politically. The very nature of the social work function entails involvement with those individuals and groups in society who have the most reason for dissatisfaction with the existing structure. And yet the role of the social worker is more than a little politically ambivalent: social workers are after all usually State employees in a State institution—can they and should they do more than act as the professional representatives of the established social order?[7] This problem opens up a wide range of themes and dilemmas—some of which will be discussed here. At this point it may suffice to outline the two major conceptions of the political role of social work which are to be discussed.

The psycho-social view of social work stresses the extent to which the client's situation results from social and general environmental influences. These factors should, according to this concept of social work, be combined with individual psychological/emotional influences to achieve a correct perspective on the client's situation. Politically, this concept of social work is often held to imply a social democratic perspective.[8]

Social work therefore can be seen as a reforming agent within

3

society, helping both individual *and* society to evolve via the social democratic parliamentary system along more socially concerned and humane lines. Thus social work acts as a legitimate pressure-group operating within the present socio-political structure and campaigning for both specific policies and a general reorientation of strategy and/or philosophy (i.e. for policies based upon a more egalitarian, redistributive system which would also be far more concerned than at present with the achievement of social justice, the extension of welfare services and the protection of the rights of the underprivileged in society generally).[9] This macro pressure-group activity can from this perspective be combined with the micro concern of continually rehabilitating individuals and demonstrating to them the potential for change through group action. This overall reformist conception of social work (which will be discussed fully in Chapter 4 in the context of the developments of the social democratic and reformist perspectives in British political culture generally) has two important implications: first, that our existing social and political structure is capable of major change in the respects outlined above, and second, that the parliamentary and other political and social institutions that at present exist, are both powerful enough and accessible enough to accomplish such changes.

It will be argued that this psycho-social reformist view of social work emphasizes its potential as a radical but integrative force within society. From this perspective the legitimation process is seen not only as a part of the inculcation of the ideology of the dominant culture: social work also has, at least potentially, the ability to become a strong professional pressure-group operating within the existing social and political institutional structure, as a genuinely radical force capable of demanding and achieving fundamental change.[10] This debate around the question of legitimation is a key area and Chapter 6 is devoted to this discussion in the context of social work.

From a Marxist perspective, society, and the function and role of social work within that society, is viewed somewhat differently. From this viewpoint the essential feature of British society (and the Western world generally) remains its basic capitalist structure. To a very large degree this structure determines the shape and nature of the social and political institutions. The ways in which British society and political culture have evolved have, according to the Marxist view, masked the essentially irrational and contradictory nature of the system. We may have a welfare-oriented capitalist system (although even this is open to major questioning), but the fundamental point about our society remains not its welfare but its capitalism. Given this sort of approach, social work must be seen as an institution of the State which exists to perpetuate an unworkable and undesirable system. Moreover, as its primary function is to 'rehabilitate' some of those elements in society which are not 'integrated', social work performs part of the invaluable task of legitimating the existing structure. Arguments stressing the importance of the legitimation process in the modern sophisticated State (as against the more familiar coercive forces) will be analysed in some detail (see Chapter 6). It is however important to note here that according to this argument social work acts institutionally as a mechanism for identifying and absorbing potential social revolt against the *status quo*. (Again, this argument is analogous to that which claims that the Labour party, far from having a radical or even potentially radical, political function, plays 'a major role in the management of discontent and helps to keep it within safe bounds . . .'.[11])

All this is not to say that Marxists are completely pessimistic about the political potential of social work: far from it. Marxists maintain, on the contrary, that if social workers would dispose of their reformist illusions and adopt a 'correct' political perspective, they could become a vital part of the revolutionary movement. These arguments and their implications for social work will be explored in Chapters 6 and 7, but it is obvious that, from this perspective, social work becomes potentially a crucial area for the revolutionary.

These then are some of the specific issues to be raised about the nature of social work in its political context. Inevitably, though, the debate involves a wider range of social and political questions and some time will be spent on both the diverse perspectives on the development of British political culture and the even more fundamental arguments about the nature and purpose of political activity itself and the relationship between the individual and society.

The authors, although both socialists, hold sharply distinguished ideological perspectives and, at one level, the book is an attempt to describe and analyse as fairly as possible two socialist (i.e. the democratic socialist and Marxist)[12] interpretations of the social work function. No attempt has been made to duck issues, or slide around disagreements, and it is perhaps surprising to note the extent of agreement between the authors over the analysis and description of the situation in which social work finds itself—even if the implicit differences over the prescription for the future of social work are somewhat more marked.

Little time is spent in arguing that social work has political connotations: the case for such an assumption appears to us so overwhelming as to need little elucidation. What is attempted is a thoroughgoing exchange of analyses and prescriptions between the differing political viewpoints. In the final chapter the argument is broadened out somewhat although social work remains the focus of attention: whilst no final agreement can be reached between the two perspectives a number of conclusions does appear possible. The links between social work and political belief are deep-rooted and influential at every level—the more so, perhaps, because they are often not consciously expressed.[13] As social work assumes greater importance within the social structure[14] so the need for a clarification of social work roles and an explicit ideological commitment becomes ever more urgent. Both the democratic socialist and the Marxist are convinced of the need for social work involvement in the wider social and political context: the nature of that involvement depends upon the arguments and assumptions of the initial analysis. It is with this dual problem—of social work practice and its relation to political ideology—that this book is fundamentally concerned. Whether social work can best help to achieve the radical changes in social and political structure (which both authors see as necessary) by adopting a 'reformist' or a 'revolutionary' perspective is by no means a simple question: the following chapters try to outline some of the arguments on either side, and will, we hope, contribute to the overdue debate on the ideological context of social work.

Chapter two

Tolerating uncertainty

Every generation has probably considered itself to be rather special and every age, modern. Change, while stimulating, has always been accompanied by some element of threat, but undoubtedly the current rate of change, with the loss of so many familiar social landmarks, has been unparalleled. Even though twentieth-century war dramatically changed the face of Europe there was evidence of some continuity, some coherence:[1] but today the pace of change and the technological developments in the armaments industry jeopardize Western civilization, and even man's ability to survive as a species is in serious question. As far as the West is concerned it is probably true to say that never before has there been such a lack of confidence in civilization's ability to survive: threatened by nuclear annihilation, the resources crisis, over-population and growing social anarchy, 'traditional values' are under constant attack.[2]

The general unease and apparent purposelessness of Western society has been proclaimed by such people as Solzhenitsyn,[3] and while there is much to criticize in his thesis, the relevance lies not so much in the accuracy or otherwise of his analysis but rather in the response to his attacks. He touched upon a whole range of semi-articulated fears and beliefs and, above all, gave expression to the prevailing feeling of social and spiritual uncertainty.

Social work inevitably reflects the society which bore it and in which it operates. Even before the accumulated growth of the profession in the 1970s, Timms, in the early 1960s, was describing social work education as a training for uncertainty.[4] The increase in socio-political writings concerning the role of social work in society, may well reflect something of the ambiguity that many feel about the profession.[5]

Paradoxically, increasing educational levels, plus the vast out-pourings of intellectual knowledge, in part explain the widespread ethos of uncertainty which has accompanied the rapid social, political and technological change of the twentieth century. Shaw discerned this development in the 1920s, complaining bitterly that the social sciences illuminated the past while leaving the present in utter darkness.[6] The danger is that practitioners, academics, experts, etc., will seek to maintain their own coherence by clinging to the established doctrines of their formative years, rather than attempting the necessary re-evaluation.

Social work, therefore, as an institution of modern society may easily lose direction and seek to perpetuate obsolescent roles: it urgently requires an analysis that will aid in the understanding of its social and political functions if it is to avoid an uncomprehending rigidity. For, as we have argued, social work is inevitably political, especially as it increasingly finds itself in the forefront of executing successive governments' social policies. Social work, as an identifiable institution, may not have a history much beyond 140 years, but its nature has changed fundamentally during that time: the early impetus for social work came from the voluntary philanthropic organizations,[7] and it acted in the main as a vehicle for the 'good works' of the private citizen. Social work today is, however, in large part, concerned with governmental or societal intervention in the lives of individual citizens. Writing of policy developments in government, Smith states that the[8]

> study of public policy-making ultimately demands an assessment of all aspects of the political system. Studies of political institutions, the machinery of government and the decision-making processes must be carried out within a framework of power as it is exercised in all social relationships.

This injunction is most pertinent as social work is now undeniably part of 'public policy-making' and of the machinery of government.[9] Perhaps less well appreciated is the fact that social work is also a part of the political and institutional structure of our society and, with the other Welfare State institutions, can be claimed by both the major political parties as part of their political and social 'weaponry': an active part of the campaign to combat society's ills, as they are variously perceived. (See, for example, the ministerial statements of both Sir Keith Joseph and David Ennals when Secretary of State at the Department of Health and Social Security.) What is perhaps unique to social work, in comparison with other welfare professions, is its potential ability to examine, and by virtue of its knowledge base,[10] predict, issues of social policy and social structure.

Social work, in its basic Certificate of Qualification in Social Work training has a mandatory sociology and social policy and administration input which equips its practitioners, from the outset, with a critical and evaluatory awareness enabling the profession to analyse, and authoritatively comment upon, social policy as it evolves via the political process.

There is, however, a tendency within 'administrative studies' of all types to concentrate upon the nuts and bolts of the way the machine works, thus ignoring what the machine is meant to be doing! In this, as in other areas we shall be stressing throughout, there is an absolute need for social work to debate the ideological context in which it operates and the various options open to it, on both the individual and collective, processional level.

The need for such an orientation has indeed been acknowledged by a former Minister at the DES[11] who urged that academic social administration should desert its traditional, but spurious, 'politically neutral' position and instead alert students to the political context in which social policy is argued. Recently, there has been a growing interest in efforts to conceptualize and unify the primary task of social work, concentrating upon purpose rather than method, which had been the predominant emphasis in the last decade.[12] In part, this has arisen as an attempt to arrive at a synthesis of the many disparate branches of social welfare activities that cluster under the umbrella term of 'social work'. Efforts have been made to integrate some of the major theoretical contributions to social work practice, in what has been described as a 'Unitary Approach'.[13] These paradigms might be better understood as an eclectic and utilitarian use of knowledge drawn from different sources and competing theories. Thus the idiosyncratic situation of the 'client' can be explored to determine which set of factors, or systems, are impinging most upon him, which contribute either to the difficulties experienced by him, or which might yield potential support or resolution of the situation. This is not the place to discuss the merits or demerits of the systems-theory advocates, though what is particularly valuable in the model for social workers is that it presents something of the complexity of the situation and enables the multi-factorial elements to be studied more easily.

Thus the social worker is able to explore alternative assessments which are possibly related to each other, and at the same time, to consider possible linkages between apparently varied aspects of the client's life. The theoretical framework is particularly attractive to British social work at present, largely because of its likely applicability to those working in multi-purpose agencies, such as social services departments. Baker[14] has developed this concept in a useful integrated way and has formulated the idea of a multi-method social worker. Nevertheless, the utilitarian development still demands a more focused analysis of the broad purposes of social work: the attempts to implement theoretical sociological frameworks have not resulted in a unified social work perspective—in either practical or theoretical terms.[15]

Another factor that may add to the uncertainty surrounding social work practice is the omnibus nature of the profession: this can be seen in a brief glance at some of the inherently contradictory legislation that social work has often to execute. For example, under the Education Act education is mandatory and must, in effect, take place in schools. The compulsory element is re-affirmed, by implication, in the Children and Young Persons Act 1969, which considers sanctions against any breach of the Education Act—yet the 1975 Children Act accepts into statute for the first time, the principle that the *child's* interest and welfare must be a major criterion to be considered by courts, even possibly against the declared wishes or interests of the parents, something hitherto unprecedented in English law.

Yet, in terms of *rights*, children are more restricted than adults: there is, after all, no mandatory place of residence or 'employment' to correspond to school for adults—except in cases concerning crime or madness!

Social work operates on a potentially anomalous footing in the whole area of 'authority': it has been argued by Butrym[16] that the 'control' and 'care' functions of social work should be seen not as conflicting but complementary. On the other hand, fears have been expressed by Jordan that given the process of stigmatization by a bureaucratized Welfare State, 'control' rather than 'care' is likely to predominate.[17]

These recent works might be said to typify something of the ambiguity of social work, for while there *appear* to be very different orientations on the *political* spectrum both Butrym and Jordan—along with writers such as Holman[18]—hold a central reformist position. However, Marxist analysts of social work—such as Pearson[19] and Leonard[20]—urge a complete re-think of the whole discipline. It might be said that Butrym and Jordan, despite their different emphases, actually share similar professional orientations, although their work demonstrates implicitly a divergence of views on wider social values. Butrym stresses the need to view social work as a 'vocation' and is on the side of the angels, while Jordan seems to view the profession as much more of a crusade (and possibly does not believe in angels) being more concerned to counter the effect of the 'big battalions'; though he would undoubtedly share Butrym's view that there is a need for personal integrity, stringency and sacrifice in the service of the client.

The differences between 'Reformist' and 'Marxist' oriented writers represent the *apparently* opposing alignments in social work: on the one hand those who see the professional concerned essentially with the individual and his family, though not denying the importance of social factors, and on the other, those who view social work primarily as a vehicle for societal change, whilst not ignoring individuals' needs. Because each side recognizes factors crucial to the other's orientation (i.e. individual and societal) there is often actual overlap in practice and a blurring of goals and aims. Not only may this confuse the outsider, it may also mislead the practitioner as to the primary objective. Nevertheless, once the fundamental ideologies, basic to the two broad positions, are pursued, the variations in the analysis and consequent action may be clearly demonstrated. The two positions divide, albeit schematically, into general political positions which will be analysed and discussed in the following chapters.

But why has social work begun to concern itself with politics now? It might be argued that this is something of a reaction in the profession to the virtual exclusion of any such debate in the 1950s and 1960s. Moreover, the realization that poverty,[21] both relative and absolute, had not been eradicated, came perhaps as a shock to the growing numbers of social workers who, brought up in boom times, believed that deceptive slogan of the late 1950s—'we have never had it so good'. Of course, during these years the social work scene was dominated, with one or two notable exceptions, by writers who were predominantly American, and whilst they might in the context of their own culture have been considered radical, they generally accepted the broad structure of American society as given, often giving implicit and even explicit support to the capitalist/ protestant ethic.[22]

In Great Britain, unlike the USA, there has been overt criticism of the political and professional *status quo*,[23] and the emergence of the magazine *Case Con.* seems to have developed along with the Marxist upsurge of the late 1960s and early 1970s. Yet how active is this militant group, how influential and how deep-rooted? It may be that when the history of this decade of social work is written it will be known as the time of the 'Political Deluge', as Woodroofe[24] described the 'Psychiatric Deluge' of the previous era. Yet Butrym[25] wryly and rightly points out, that social work in this earlier period may well have been dominated by the *writings* of the 'psychiatric' and ego-dynamically oriented caseworkers, but in practice such social work probably operated in only a few areas. (This has been confirmed by Gath and his colleagues[26] who found little change in the traditional casework orientation of the Child Guidance Clinic, compared with Timms's survey in the mid-1960s[27] where the majority of work undertaken with clients was of short duration.)

Whether the political radicals *should* have a major influence on social work practice and objectives forms a central concern of this book. This question, and indeed the whole ethos of uncertainty which surrounds social work and other social institutions, is related to fundamental questions concerning values and ideology. Before we turn to look at the ways in which ideological systems have emerged in Britain through the 'political culture', we must first consider some of the questions relating to values in social work.

Values in social work and society

Social work cannot exist without a value framework or frameworks to operate by: as judgments entail values, the objective non-judgmental stance so often advocated for social work is by definition untenable.

Values are the qualitative base that underpin human interactions and transactions—for the social worker they are said to be 'matters of living reality since he will continually come up against them in the course of his daily work'.[28] They are therefore the moral foundations of practice and social work is indebted to Plant[29] for his linking of moral theory to one major branch of social work method: social casework. He shows clearly that the moral standpoint directly affects, amongst other things, the political perspective of the worker, since the social work role, as with other functional roles, has implicit moral connotations. Traditionally, the West has centred concepts of morality upon Christian ethics, and for many this perspective has given impetus to their commitment to the profession.[30]

However, with the dramatic and widespread decline in religious influence, a new, humanist ethos has emerged to form the basis of the perceived value system of British society. This system, founded upon a sort of secular Christianity, is rarely enunciated positively or fully: various aspects of the liberal tradition are stressed by different people at different times but the whole package is somehow assumed to be almost intuitive and not requiring elucidation or analysis.[31] Nevertheless, there is a cluster of values which is held to be central to the existence of Western liberal democratic society, and to Britain in particular: the primary importance of the individual, a parliamentary democratic system of government, participation and responsibility across the whole range of social and political institutions, freedom of communication, equality before the law, an independent judiciary, and a social welfare system based upon the protection of the weak—these form some of the basic liberal beliefs about society.[32] One of the crucial questions over which the ideologies differ is the extent to which these objectives are realized, or indeed are realizable, within the existing social system. Social workers, by and large without much conscious debate, accept these liberal assumptions about society and social values: in later chapters, particularly in Chapter 6 where we discuss the concept of legitimation, we shall be examining the relevance and validity of these liberal assumptions.[33] As far as social work is concerned there can be little doubt that the liberal value system has, at least until recently, remained largely unchallenged: the individualist ethic has dominated much social work literature and the desirability of participation and responsibility is being increasingly stressed.[34]

The tension between this commitment to the liberal freedom of the individual and the social worker's role as an intervening societal agent is highlighted by Jordan:[35]

> [The] notion of intervention into the lives of others can be looked at as interference with another's freedom: it can also be looked at as an obligation on every citizen as part of the web of reciprocal social duties which themselves constrain freedom.

This is interestingly paralleled by the British Association of Social Workers statement on values which contains an important qualification:[36]

> basic to the profession of social work is the recognition of the value and dignity of every human being irrespective of origin, status, sex, age, belief or contribution to society. The profession accepts responsibility to encourage and facilitate the self-realisation of the individual person *with due regard for the interests of others* [our italics].

This dual dilemma, of freedom from interference, freedom from being obliged, and freedom for the individual, versus freedom for the group, runs throughout virtually the whole of social work practice. The Biesteckian principle of 'client self-determination' is postulated as a bulwark against the invasion of the person and the promotion of positive freedoms.[37] It is also at the core of the political debate concerning 'necessary' constraints that go to make up the governance of a society.

How these tensions within social work practice can be lessened is ultimately dependent upon the ideological assumptions made about both social work and about general social structure and development.

There are, of course, other wide areas of disagreement in social work—most notably perhaps about the psychological and physiological nature of man: these cannot concern us here but they are of crucial importance for the profession. In our context we shall try to focus upon the ideological and political divisions which give rise to differing perceptions of social work, but in addition to these divisions and conflicts it is important to remember the major uncertainties surrounding social work theory and practice in other fields.

Professional confusion: personal crisis?

If social work, be it a profession, a discipline or simply an occupation, is so beset with uncertainties what motivates people to become social workers? The cynic might reply that the answer lies in the advent of the social services departments, with the proliferation of well paid jobs—but this is a superficial assessment: such affluence as there is, is a very recent development—prior to this social workers were very poorly rewarded (and, indeed, many still remain so).

Whatever the individual's motivation—to help those in need, or to achieve social change—there can be no doubt that 'society' has seen an increasing need for social work agencies over the last two decades.[38]

Despite the *ad hoc* nature of the legal framework, the State has affirmed since 1945 its intention to care for the elderly, the sick, the handicapped and the family (i.e. family/child welfare) as a major *thematic* responsibility. Also those 'Community Health Care' responsibilities previously executed by the old Medical Officer of Health (such as mental illness and handicap and the chronic sick within the community) are now under a unified authority, and might be broadly divided into 'Community Health Care' and Child and Family Welfare Services. (We are indebted to Alan Tredenick for the development of the idea of 'general specialisms' under the appropriate statutes as organized in his area directorate in Bath, Avon Social Services Department.)

The expansion of social work, is, of course, a part of the major development of the Welfare State, but in the specific social work context there is a fundamental tension between the role of social worker as agent of social change and the controlling role as envisaged by the institutional establishment.[39] In an uncharacteristically blunt part of their report, the Central Council for Training and Education in Social Work enjoined social workers to explore[40]

> the assumptions about either equality or income differentials which need careful and informed debate in social work education. Social workers have a dual commitment to concern for individuals on the one side and to the social care structure of society on the other. So, while keeping the immediate welfare of their clients at the forefront of their concern they must consider the place of social work within the structure of a *capitalist society of which they are a part* [our italics].

Controversy is inevitable: however insistent the claim of any group to have the 'gospel', there will be a 'Non-conformist' opposition to point to an alternative. Many directors of social services must echo Shaw's King Magnus[41] in their feeling of inevitably offending one group by implementing the ideas of another. In Shaw's words—'For some people, not to belong to the Church of England [read Florence Hollis] means that you are not quite respectable—for another, to belong to the Anglican persuasion [read Eysenck] means you are damned'!

Unfortunately, rational, informed, authoritative guidance is not really possible. It might be expected from the social work educational field but even here uncertainty reigns. This is partly due to the speed of the structural change within social work itself, and partly to the fact that the majority of teachers are more familiar with a style of practice that is either unfashionable or hardly feasible in the multi-purpose agencies that have developed. Because there is no unified framework for either social work practice or societal analysis within social work, the teacher will always be at variance with at least some of his students, some of the time. This is further compounded by the varied tasks given to social work by various legislative enactments. There is a vague public confidence which has enabled this delegation of power to take place, but there is no general social and political appreciation of what the sum total of this power implies or could imply—by either 'the public' or the profession. Many social work students emerge from the social sciences armed with critical insights into the defects of societal superstructure, often valid and useful, plus enthusiastic idealism. But the student is often trapped by the desire for certainty and frustrated by the awareness of the 'macro' task he has undertaken, with all its accompanying uncertainties.

Clashes in the perception of social work roles—for example, between social services committees and professional social workers in the field as well as between social workers themselves—are almost inevitable in a situation where there are no commonly agreed social work theories or goals. Again this is a problem that can be resolved only by a conscious debate over social work 'ideology'.

But to return to the motivations of individual social workers. In the main, we would argue, social workers are motivated by vocational impetus in response to deeply held, if often unarticulated, values. It is this fuzziness about a central value system plus the mounting attack on the ideological values of 'liberal capitalism', both in social work and in society generally, that has contributed in large measure to the differences and hostilities between different groups within social work. These differences often produce what might be described as the 'heresy response' as each party accuses the other of 'deviating from the truth'; as in traditional religious heretical situations, the most wounding aspect of the disagreement is the sense of betrayal by someone you assumed was of your 'party'. The feeling of betrayal comes partly from the fact that values held by contending parties usually overlap and each makes the deduction that both are operating from the same premises—and in fact this may often be the case, with different conclusions being drawn from the same set of hypotheses.[42] We are thus left in a situation where motivation appears to be vocational, deeply felt and yet confused. One of the major roots of this confusion lies, we shall argue, in the lack of a clearly formulated ideological framework for interpreting both social work and the wider social structure.

Such a situation, however, might not seem to be so serious in a new profession seeking to understand itself and to comprehend its role in relation to the people it serves and the rest of society. But there are important practical results: it is now recognized that the debate surrounding values directly affects social work practice and priorities. And at a time of stringency and battles for resources such a disparate response can only weaken or dissipate the 'common front'—and social work administrators are increasingly finding that they have to defend concepts, policies and social priorities that had been thought secure since the post-1945 'commitment to welfare.'[43]

There can be no doubt that our present age is one of uncertainty:[44] old values, especially the religious, have been largely cast aside and yet no new coherent and cohesive framework of beliefs has, in the West, been adopted in their place. There is a prevailing sense of drift, of purposelessness, and a fatalistic reaction to the ever-increasing pace of change.

Within this uncertain macrocosmic context social work is, not unsurprisingly, beset by doubt, dissent and lack of direction. Social workers as individuals have different perspectives on how social work should function, on what its objectives should be and so on, often because they differ in their wider ideological assumptions.

It is thus necessary to look in some detail at the nature and explanation of this ideological division. Through a study of British political culture we hope to arrive at a clearer formulation of the alternative frameworks within which social work methods and objectives are themselves formulated.

Chapter three

Political culture of contemporary Britain (1): Conservatism

Introduction

Social work originated neither autonomously nor in a social or political vacuum. Similarly social work cannot operate independently of social and political factors in contemporary society. Given these assumptions, it becomes important for social workers to have a clear understanding of the varying perceptions on social and political structure, not only because this gives a more comprehensive view of society that is generally useful, but also because such understanding is essential for directly professional reasons. Unless social workers understand both the historical - ideological framework from which social work grew, and, perhaps more importantly, the major ideological perspectives within which social workers operate, they will be unable to cope with the underlying political considerations inherent in social work practice.

As we noted earlier (Chapter 1) politics is concerned centrally with issues of power in society: how *is* power distributed and how *ought* power to be distributed? What are the relationships between these 'power' questions and questions of, for example, economics and social structure? And, in the context of social work, perhaps the most important question of all: how do political/social attitudes relate to political/social structure?

Social work is concerned, intimately and fundamentally, with both the pragmatic and the conceptual aspects of these power questions. Pragmatically—with party attitudes to social work and its financing, with the Welfare State, with the extension of benefits to the less well-off and so on. More subtly, and more importantly, social work is deeply involved with questions of political culture. Political culture is concerned 'less (with) the formal and informal structures of politics, governments, parties, pressure groups and so on, or the actual pattern of political behaviour observed within a

Political culture of contemporary Britain (1): Conservatism

society, but rather (with) what people *believe* about those structures and behaviours'.[1] It is concerned, in other words, with subjective perceptions rather than objective analysis. For social workers this is of crucial importance as it is from within the varying ideological contexts[2] that attitude formation crystallizes. 'Political culture', then, is important across a wide range of areas, ranging from deviance (e.g. why does 'society' regard sexual deviance as dangerous and anti-social?), through poverty studies (e.g. why does contemporary society find it impossible, or undesirable, to eradicate the substantial poverty that remains?), to macro-political questions (e.g. which, if any, of the major ideological perspectives provides the best chance of eradicating or substantially decreasing the problems that social workers have to cope with?).

There is, or should be, a twofold process at work here for social workers: a wide-ranging understanding of the various perspectives and the motivations of people who work within them, and an analytical exercise undertaken by each individual social worker to determine the most acceptable ideological framework. Ultimately, social workers, like everyone else, have to decide upon an ideological framework within which to analyse experience, but the prior exercise of a subjective understanding of the whole range of attitudes is of crucial importance in the professional context. Empathy and analysis are the twin tools required by social workers. (To pretend that social work is non-ideological of course leads to the implicit, and often unconscious, adoption of one of the most uncompromising ideological stances of all!)

It is because of this dual need that we are devoting this chapter and Chapter 4 to a study of *political culture* rather than political theory. The intention is to combine an intellectually rigorous analysis with an account of the subjective motivations contained within each perspective.

Our own perspectives will, of course, influence the analysis: there can be no objective, value-free political analysis and anyone who argues to the contrary is either a fool or a knave (or more probably both!). We have tried to give a balanced account of Conservative ideology—in fact, to get inside the collective head of British Conservatism, although our own positions are both well to the Left. The substantive argument between our two perspectives— fundamentally between the democratic socialist and Marxist viewpoints— is held over until the final chapter.

Given this dual aim it is essential to combine the contemporary with the historical. No analysis of the contemporary situation can be satisfactory without a discussion of the historical conditions in which the various frameworks developed. The discussion will thus begin by outlining the historical formation of the now dominant frameworks

Political culture of contemporary Britain (1): Conservatism

and then progress to an exposition of contemporary attitudes in the light of this historical background.

Whilst the main burden of these two chapters is concerned with the exploration of the ideas, policies and outlooks of the two dominant ideological perspectives in contemporary British society, we also see the very different analysis offered by the Marxist framework as being crucial to a proper understanding. To accept too readily the subjective, and therefore inevitably partisan, accounts of the protagonists of Conservatism and social democracy without offering a critical analysis from a divergent viewpoint would be a serious omission. Moreover, both authors, despite their different ideological standpoints, agree that Marxist analysis of contemporary political culture is crucial to a full understanding. The questions raised by Marxist analysis concerning the nature and purpose of social and political change are at the forefront of the debate in social work over methods and objectives. Unlike the other two perspectives discussed, Marxism posits an explanation which, if accepted, demands radical and controversial changes across the whole range of social, economic and political relationships and structures. Marxism claims that neither the Conservative nor the social democratic frameworks question the fundamentals of the capitalist system. Moreover, social democrats as much as Conservatives have a framework where problems and their solutions are placed in an *ad hoc*, pragmatic context. Marxists, in other words, claim to have not only a 'more correct' but a 'more fully developed' analysis. We have therefore appended to both this chapter on Conservatism and to Chapter 4 a section outlining a Marxist analysis.

The frameworks we are discussing are essentially *ideological* frameworks: that is, they can all be described as systems of thought and analysis for defining social reality.[3] They are concerned therefore only in part with traditional political structure—they include not only institutional structures, party politics and so on, but also the wider conceptual frameworks of interpretation that are used for social and political policy-making and value judgments. One of the hallmarks of an important ideological framework is its flexibility in terms of appeal and sophistication. (Hence the ability of both Catholicism and Communism to appeal on both the 'higher' levels of intellectual sophistication and the 'lower' levels of quasi-peasant simplicity.) Thus, even amongst the national leadership of the Labour Party in the UK, one finds right-wing social democrats (e.g. in recent Labour Party history, George Brown and Anthony Crosland) who, to put it politely, cover a wide range of the intellectual spectrum, supporting almost identical policy lines.[4]

This point—the generality of these frameworks—needs emphasis particularly because the frameworks in question (Conservative and

Political culture of contemporary Britain (1): Conservatism

Liberal/Social Democratic) appear on first sight to be explicitly political in the conventional sense. But in reality they are also indicative of a much wider commitment (often unconscious) to particular ideological interpretations of society—and it is in this wider sense that we shall be discussing the problems.

One final introductory point—the analysis of political culture is a major undertaking and given the limited scope of this book the treatment given here is necessarily brief.[5] This brevity may appear to lead to an over-schematic approach: why *should* these frameworks be accepted as encapsulating the various perspectives currently held in social and political culture? To some extent this is a valid criticism—there are some viewpoints, or semi-isolated schools of thought on particular issues, which do not fall easily within these frameworks. But we would maintain that as far as the ideological mainstream goes the vast majority of individuals and institutions in the UK would subscribe to one or the other, to a greater or lesser degree consciously. (And this applies not only to specifically political organizations: the media, the education system, the churches and so on all fall within this spectrum.)

The purpose, then, of this chapter is to outline the development and contemporary nature of British political culture, before relating these various perspectives specifically to social work.

Conservatism

Appropriately, we begin with Conservatism—by far the oldest and most consistently successful of the ideological systems *and*, for most Conservatives far more important, the focus for the most longstanding and successful of British political parties. 'Despite major changes in British society, major threats from rivals apparently better able to champion popular interests, the Conservative phoenix has always hitherto been reborn from the ashes of defeat.'[6] Unlike the other frameworks we are discussing Conservatives have traditionally been doubtful about the value of political activity and have consistently seen Conservatism's ideological message as being far wider than 'mere politics'. Quintin Hogg (now Lord Hailsham, again) vigorously defended this aspect of Conservatism in one of the few modern works on Conservative *attitudes*.[7]

> Conservatives do not believe that political struggle is the most important thing in life. In this they differ from Communists, Socialists, Nazis, Fascists, Social Creditors and most members of the British Labour Party. The simplest among them prefer fox-hunting—the wisest, religion. To the great majority of

Political culture of contemporary Britain (1): Conservatism

> Conservatives, religion, art, study, family, country, friends, music, fun, duty, all the joys and riches of existence of which the poor no less than the rich are the indefeasible freeholders, all these are higher in the scale than their handmaiden, the political struggle . . . The man who puts politics first is not fit to be called a civilized being, let alone a Christian . . . .

This seemingly apolitical view of life—and indeed of politics—finds its reflection in social work as elsewhere. In this view politics is construed as essentially the process of governing:[8] the governors of society need of course to be expert at the art of government, but they also need the all-round qualities of the archetypal Renaissance man who can take an intelligent and civilized interest in all aspects of life and who has experience of a wide range of interests and occupations. For Conservatives, the art of governing is in fact heavily dependent upon acquiring, through 'specialised preparatory training . . . a habit of mind'—not a vocational training but 'rather . . . an ability to handle men and affairs that depends more on character than on knowledge'.[9]

This traditional Conservative view is highly patrician in origin: the governing strata of society (Conservatives, of course, never use terminology like 'the ruling class') have a vocation dependent not upon wealth but upon social location. To be sure, the argument runs, this position conveys privileges but it also carries onerous social and political duties. Hence the traditional Conservative self-portrait: the civilized, responsible and humane all-rounder—drawn from an established ruling élite group, expert in his amateurism, experienced in life and therefore fit to provide tolerant and wise government, and yet very conscious of the principles of *noblesse oblige*. The implications of this perspective are that politics should be left to those who understand it—and whose social function it is to govern. The appeal of this approach (i.e. of leaving government to those whose experience, ability and social position qualify them uniquely for political power), combined with the inherent social stability which Conservatism stands for, should not be underrated when analysing the reasons for the remarkable persistence and success of the Conservative perspective.

The humanitarian strain within Conservatism is deep-rooted and genuine. The traditions of public service, self-sacrifice, team-spirit and indeed 'playing the game' are now so thoroughly discredited and unfashionable that it may be difficult for those born since the Second World War to take them seriously—not because the values are inherently worthless but rather because of the demonstrable hypocrisy which has so often accompanied their advocacy. From pre-industrial times, however, the concern of the ruling élite for the welfare of the poor has been evident.[10] From Disraeli to Macmillan there is a concern, often carried into positive, legislative action, for social welfare within the particular framework of Conservative thinking; although there must, admittedly, be doubts about the commitment of either Mr Heath or Mrs Thatcher to this aspect of the Conservative tradition.

This, then, is the basis of the Conservative's self-image of disinterested leadership and the need for an apolitical style. This is, too, the most popular view of Conservatism—a harking back to the (supposedly) golden days of the stable, rural structure before the industrial revolution. In terms of the subjective feelings of members of the Party and of large sections of the population as a whole (especially in rural areas) this is an enormously important part of the 'Conservative idea' of society. Yet it is fundamentally inadequate as an account of modern Conservatism, which is dominated by a very different credo to the subjugation, though not the exclusion, of the 'Old Tory' ideas just outlined.

In his excellent work on British politics[11] Samuel Beer emphasizes the Conservatives' continuous and continuing belief in order and hierarchy; indeed he opens the 'Old Tory' section of his work with this quotation from *Troilus and Cressida* used by Sir John Anderson in the House of Commons in 1947:[12]

Take but degree away, untune that string,
And hark, what discord follows!

In the sixteenth century and early seventeenth century the concept of a cosmic order was dominant. The cosmic hierarchy extended to terrestrial as well as heavenly arrangements: only through the hierarchical structure could order and stability be assured. Moreover, it was argued that this hierarchical structure, corresponding to universal laws, was God-given, and thus any attempt to change or undermine the social order was, by definition, an attack on God and therefore not only politically but morally indefensible. There was thus a premium on the maintenance of the legal, social and political *status quo*. This respect for the existing social hierarchy at any given period—the instinct to conserve rather than reform—has remained an important part of Conservatism long after the religious justification for such a perspective had passed.

From this aspect of Conservatism comes one of its strongest appeals: its psychological attraction. The Conservative rhetorical emphasis upon pragmatism, continuity, 'playing safe' and the principle of conservation rather than reform, is based upon the sound psychological assumption that most people prefer the 'devil they know'. Change is seen as 'theoretical', 'unreal', 'academic' and so on. Perspectives of reform are, therefore, seen as dangerous and misguided whilst Conservatism offers the reassurance of the familiar, the already experienced.

Contemporary psychological studies have demonstrated the 'inertial conservatism' of man which leads to docile and accepting attitudes across a wide cross-section of the population.[13] This, in turn, has contributed to the desire for continuity, which was strikingly demonstrated in 1970 when 18-year-olds in Britain were first enfranchised. Many newspaper pundits admired Harold Wilson's apparent coup of capturing the 'youth vote'—which was assumed to be predominantly 'idealistic' and therefore likely to go in Labour's favour. In reality, the 18-21-year-old voters responded in similar voting patterns to their elders. Perhaps if Harold Wilson had looked at modern psychological research he would have been less sanguine. Offer and Offer[14] found that young people generally share the same political and social attitudes as their parents—and indeed are as depressing a carbon copy as any party manager could wish for. This is perhaps one of the reasons that subjective attitudinal changes about society occur so slowly, while the 'real' world of hierarchy and pressures for social conformity, even in the notoriously non-conforming adolescent, maintain the stability of the existing structure.

The emphasis upon stability and hierarchy forms the basis of modern Conservatism. The original hierarchical perspective of 'Old Toryism' found its secular justification in the eighteenth century, particularly in the thoughts of Burke.[15] There must, according to Burke, be a governing group in any form of society and this group must consist of 'the wiser, the more expert, and the more opulent [whose function is to] enlighten and protect the weaker, the less knowing and the less provided with the goods of the future'. Only this aristocratic ruling élite had the knowledge, the experience, and, in the literal sense, the breeding to use reason to solve society's problems.

Implicit in Burke's concept of society as an organic whole evolving gradually and continuously through time is the crucial idea of rationality that has underlain much of liberal and later social democratic thinking as well as conservatism.[16] This argument holds that, objectively, society is a potentially unified whole with shared assumptions and perspectives: if this assumption is granted then it follows that there can be one, and only one, rational answer to a given problem. Social conflict, or the clash of perspectives which give rise to social conflict, is thus the result of irrationality, ignorance or selfishness. If the most able people are in control and if sufficient patience is exercised in discussions and explanations of policies in sensitive areas, then rationality will triumph and social conflict diminish.

Political culture of contemporary Britain (1): Conservatism

This argument (the antithesis of the Marxist basis of social analysis) underlies the post-1945 consensus view of politics. Indeed, the 'rationality' argument underlies the whole ethos of mainstream political and social attitudes in the twentieth century,[17] whereby problems are seen as soluble by a mixture of explanation and the isolation of men of 'ill-will' (i.e. 'subversives', 'enemies of the State', and so on). The emphasis here is on the national (as opposed to class or group) interest; on the unity (rather than the division) of society; and on moderation and persuasion (not 'extremism' and conflict). Running parallel to this 'rationality' perspective has been, of course, the more widely recognized Conservative belief in the need for hard bargaining to reach an acceptable compromise. Conservatives have always been ready to adapt—sometimes even reverse—their ideological stance in order to maintain political power and stability. But this readiness to bargain is not in conflict with the 'rationality principle'; the one rational solution will be arrived at through a process of argument, negotiation and 'give-and-take' between men of good-will. It is only the men of 'ill-will' (those who reject the 'prevailing common sense' to use Gramsci's phrase) who will refuse to participate in this process.

So far then we have isolated some of the earlier and more general, but still extant, aspects of Conservatism: its inherent belief in order, hierarchy and the *status quo*; its equally strong convictions of social unity and the need for a governing élite; its psychological appeal to order and stability on the one hand and the security of the familiar on the other; and its insistence upon a uniquely British mixture of the attributes of the amateur gentleman with those of the Renaissance man, for the members of the governing élite.

How did this framework of beliefs—this definable ideological position—become transposed into the industrial age of the nineteenth and twentieth centuries? How did Britain's ruling élite—among whose major defining characteristics had been their ties with the land—become transformed, within the political vehicle of the Conservative party, into the predominantly industrial/managerial élite of the mid-twentieth century? How, in effect, did Conservatism change from the dominant ideological framework of the landed gentry of an agrarian society into one of the two major ideological frameworks of nineteenth- and twentieth-century industrial England?

In a sense one has to look no further than Peel and Disraeli. This is not an attempt at a general political history and anyone interested in the detailed events of the post-1846 period which was so crucial for the Conservative party is advised to consult the books recommended in the Bibliography. Nevertheless, the 1846 crisis of identity and the later impact of Disraelian ideas and organization are crucial for an understanding of twentieth-century Conservatism.

Political culture of contemporary Britain (1): Conservatism

By the Repeal of the Corn Laws in 1846[18] Peel brought to a head the inherent conflict of loyalties within Conservatism. Founded on the seemingly timeless interests of the agrarian ruling élite, the landed aristocracy and the squirearchy, the Conservative Party was confronted with rapid industrialization and the enormous social changes—not least in terms of economic and political power—which this heralded. Either it maintained its traditional alliance with social groups who were becoming increasingly tangential to the centres of political and economic power, or it amended its policies and ideology to attract the new influential social groups into its ranks.[19] The Tory Party's greatest single asset has always been its instinct for survival and its ability to adapt as necessary to preserve its position as the 'political representative' of the ruling groups in society. In this case, therefore, it is hardly surprising that the Party eventually revoked its alliance with the land, and by adopting Free Trade policies came into ideological line with the new social forces of entrepreneurial capitalism. This was a major ideological watershed for the Conservative Party: although the immediate effect was to divide the Tories into Peelites, reformers and traditional landed Tories, by the end of the nineteenth century the Party had become 'the party of all the rich'.[20]

The crisis is also indicative of a number of major permanent traits of the Conservative idea: the adaptation to the spirit of the age and the consequent rejection of nostalgic, reactionary and above all *unrealistic* appeals to a previous golden age; the pragmatism and distaste for 'theory'—reacting to rather than shaping the socio-political environment; and, as already noted, the Party's inherent ability to survive by drastic adaptation when necessary.[21]

The Conservative ideological framework thus changed during the middle of the nineteenth century from the old, paternalistic, Burkean Conservatism to a new, more liberal perspective. How did this perspective differ from the old Tory framework? From an analytical point of view the Conservatism of the later nineteenth century is characterized by its ability, through flexibility and compromise, to effect an alliance between the landed aristocracy and the new powerful group of industrial capitalists to maintain social and political power based on the old principles of order and hierarchy.[22] From the subjective stance of those working for and believing in Conservatism events appeared rather differently. Disraelian (and Randolph Churchillian) concepts of Tory democracy preserved the paternalist link between the rulers and the common people: implicit in Tory thinking was the idea that whilst universal (male) suffrage would inevitably come about, government, and thus power, must remain in the hands of those with expertise and experience. In the new social environment, Disraeli argued, the leaders of society could maintain a national identity only if 'there was a proper national ideology which encompassed the population and was defined by the leadership and if the leadership demonstrated concretely that it cared for the led by introducing welfare provisions and reform'.[23] The provision of welfare services was seen by Disraeli as the major plank of the Conservatives' 'social contract'. 'The maintenance of the poor is a social duty, a duty justified by high state policy and consecrated by the sanctity of religion.'[24] And these objectives were put into practice, to some extent, in the legislation of the 1870s.[25]

An even more important aspect of the new strategy developed by Disraeli and pursued by later Conservatives in the nineteenth and twentieth centuries, centred on two interrelated aspects of the 'national idea'—the monarchy and the Empire. Whatever the structural reasons underlying the vast expansion of British imperialism in the last quarter of the nineteenth century, there was an undeniable vigour in the way in which Disraeli, and later Salisbury, promulgated the idea of British world hegemony as an extension of the domestic situation where the civilized, service-oriented, ruling élite governed in the interest of the whole nation. The world mission of the British was held to lie in the spread of the British system (of justice, of government, of morality, of behaviour—in short of society) across the world. From the outset this role was described in Kiplingesque terms—the 'white man's burden' approach to Empire. There was much rhetoric of service and of bringing Christianity to the barbarians and yet, as so often with Conservatism, this was combined with a hard-headed Realpolitik.[26] Whether or not Lenin and later Marxists have been correct in attributing the fundamental dynamic of imperialism to the development of 'monopoly capitalism', there is no doubt that for political reasons, the Conservatives were eager to make Empire a key part of their programme in order to promote the idea of national unity. The emphasis was upon the unity *and superiority* of the British as an integrated whole, and not on the deficiencies and conflicts within Britain itself. By stressing the imperial idea Conservatives were thus able to assert their role as patriotic defenders of the nation (as opposed to their opponents who were held to be concerned only with divisive, sectional, class warfare politics). Moreover, it gave an ideal unifying rallying call with which 'the masses' could identify *and* it appealed to the deep-rooted racial prejudice of the British working class.

It is an unpalatable fact that the prevailing popularity of 'Jingoism' has some psychological benefit in that it allows identification with a strong and 'superior' in-group.[27] In the later decades of the nineteenth century, when British supremacy was being challenged both economically and politically by European rivals, and when domestic social structure was under severe strain, there was abiding comfort in the concept of a secure and stable Empire presided over by the seemingly everlasting Queen Victoria. No matter how hard-pressed at home, both the bourgeois and the proletarian could identify with the British Empire and take pride in their 'natural superiority' over the (predominantly black and 'heathen') colonials. The roots of the twentieth-century Alf Garnetts indeed lie in the Tory imperialism of the late nineteenth century!

We have dwelt at some length on Disraeli because in a very real sense he created the modern Conservative Party; following on from Peel's rejection of the total identification with the land, Disraeli brought the Party to terms with the modern industrial age and its concomitant political structure. Moreover, he provided—in social reform and Empire—two broad policy issues around which the traditional Tory ideology could be reformed. As Harris puts it: 'Disraeli's significance . . . lies in the transition he made between what was left of Toryism, an incipiently counter-revolutionary doctrine for the restoration of a traditional agrarian society, to Conservatism, a position much less clearly distinguished from Liberalism.'[28]

By the early 1900s this transition was complete: 'the Conservatives were the party, not just of the land, but of the rich in general; the business man, the banker, and the financier as well as the country squire and the broadacred peer.'[29] Increasingly, from 1900, the Conservatives have been dominated by the emergent managerial and financial élites of twentieth-century capitalism.[30] Whether this new Conservatism is seen as representing the interests of the whole nation, uncluttered by sectional class interests, or as a unified attempt by all sections of the ruling class to exercise political power, depends upon the overall perspective adopted.

Certainly, the self-image of the Conservative Party in the twentieth century has been as the defender of the freedom of the individual against the 'all-powerful State'. The centralization and bureaucratization of the economic system resulted in an economic and social collectivism which the Conservatives have at times opposed vehemently in individualistic rhetoric (but have rarely opposed in policy terms when in office). Conservatives have thus come full circle from their nineteenth-century position (where they opposed the individualism of early Benthamite Liberalism and argued for stronger centralized control) and now defend the individual against the encroachment of the omnipotent State. Conservative thinkers see this not as any inconsistency but as the preservation of a moderate, sensible middle course:[31]

> Thus, although Conservatives have always supported a strong central authority when the danger to order has consisted in too much decentralization, today they believe that it could be an

evil day for Britain, and for freedom, if all power fell into the hands of the Cabinet . . . the whole outlook and philosophy of the Labour Movement can be summed up in the single phrase 'Concentration of Power' . . . Conservatives believe that the deliberate policy of concentrating more and yet more power in the hands of the executive is to jump from the frying-pan into the fire.

Incidentally, it is worth noting that the individualist rhetoric of the Conservative Party finds a sympathetic response from the social work profession which has always had a strong individualist ethic: from Mary Richmond through Biesteck to Jordan, there has been a consistent concentration on humane concerns. The social worker with experience of the large, centralized agency will find much of appeal in Hogg's thesis: social workers often feel hampered and frustrated by bureaucratic and impersonal structures where the needs of the individual client are too often forgotten.

This stress on individualism is a demonstration of one of the central features of both historical and contemporary Conservatism's self-image; the notion that the Conservative framework with its long traditions and experience, is able to steer a sensible, pragmatic, moderate course—too mature to be led astray by social or political fads of the moment, too pragmatic to be tempted into abstraction, and too conscious of heritage and continuity to try to reform too quickly. Conservatism, it is argued, represents a mature, civilized approach to politics and to the world: 'youngsters of 20' may be idealistic Socialists but by the time they reach 40 the 'realities of life' and the onset of maturity and responsibility will have convinced them, with R. A. Butler, that politics is indeed the 'Art of the Possible'.[32]

This is the subjective view. Objectively, as we have argued, Conservatism may be seen as representing the interests in the political arena of whichever groups are dominant in society over a given period of time.

Contemporary Conservatism

Given this sort of analysis of historical and attitudinal perspectives of Conservatism, what is the nature of contemporary Conservatism? Its self-image remains a mixture of the individualist, anti-collectivist (and of course anti-socialist) crusade, and an insistence upon the Disraelian concept of national unity ('the party for *all* the people'). In recent times, the party under Mrs Thatcher has reverted to an impassioned and strangely nineteenth-century appeal to *laissez-faire* individualism of a fairly full-blooded variety. Not only are the appeals for a return to a more 'private enterprise' oriented society far more than the lip-service rituals made by Edward Heath and his predecessors,[33] the overall political and economic analysis is decidedly 'anti-State capitalist'.[34]

This latest trend is too recent to bear detailed analysis (and of course at the time of writing has yet to be put to the acid test of political power), but it is interesting to note that since 1970 the Conservatives have been pursuing an ideology out of keeping in a variety of ways with the general twentieth-century development. Nigel Harris has demonstrated conclusively[35] that since 1945 the Conservative Party has been increasingly dominated by those who have accepted, and indeed ultimately welcomed, the close involvement of the State in the capitalist system—and who have seen government as the key, central factor in a corporate system of economic and political management (termed by Harris the 'étatiste corporatist'). Quintessentially, these are the managerial Conservatives who conceive of politics as a managerial exercise where the rules and norms of industrial bureaucracies can be transcribed into the political system. This group based their political perspectives on the realization that capitalism had developed into a complex, centralized system in which the State had a vital role to play; further they realized that the major challenge to the profitability and efficiency of capitalism lay in the organized Labour Movement and its ability to press for higher wage levels (and better social services, etc.). Hence the strategy, throughout the 1950s and 1960s, of basing all policies on the assumption of economic growth; most important of all, the increase in economic growth would enable wage levels to rise (in real terms) each year. The potential for institutionalized conflict between capital and labour would thus be considerably reduced as workers 'reaped the benefits of capitalism'.

The shift towards this 'étatiste corporatist' perspective came about more by force of circumstance than design. The old 'liberal', individualist Conservatism, stressing the rights of small business and the non-interference of the State and its attendant bureaucracy, was found to be simply impracticable in the conditions of the mid-twentieth century. Harris, writing of the Conservative government in the early 1960s says:[36]

> Initially, Conservatives stressed a pluralistic society: wages, nationalized industries, private firms, Government expenditure, local authority expenditure, were all to be autonomous, disciplined into an efficient whole by the overall control of a market. One by one, the State found it necessary to seek to limit that autonomy. Public expenditure and (particularly) investment had to be controlled to combat inflation, and so the

nationalized industries' finances had to be centrally scrutinized. In the field of wages, public employment had to be controlled; to do this required extensive intervention in the existing system of collective bargaining. The elements of the public sector had to act as price and wage leaders for the whole economy or compensate for the deficiencies of the private sector. Outside the public sector, wages and business coordination provided key targets for attempts at State control. Finally, planning—as an aspiration—sought to encompass all these elements into one State-supervised whole. The State as a minimum regulating agency had become both a participating system and a control system.

Given the overwhelming pressure for the 'étatiste' view, it became crucial that the cornerstone of State involvement—the continuance of economic growth—was maintained. Hence the priority given to any measure which might promote growth in a fundamentally flagging economy: investment grants, productivity incentives, the National Economic Development Council, etc.

The high point of this strategy lay in European economic federation in the European Economic Community: Edward Heath, the prime exponent of growth-oriented Conservatism, regarded the opportunities for continued capitalist expansion as resting very heavily on Britain's entry into the EEC.

On the social policy front the 'étatiste' view was also well-entrenched. Just how far the party had come along the 'planning road' can be seen in some of its social policy documents—not least those written by the two arch protagonists of traditional Toryism, Enoch Powell and Sir Keith Joseph. (Powell in 1963 in his *Health and Welfare, the Development of Community Care*, and Joseph's Green Paper *The Reorganisation of the National Health Service*, 1972.) Whether or not one agrees with the content of these policy statements (or their feasibility in terms of resources) is largely irrelevant in this context: the crucial point is that planning and centralized State administration was seen as vital for these and other policy documents.

The tactics employed to achieve these strategic aims were essentially conciliatory, rather than conflict-oriented, as has generally been the case with the Conservative Party throughout the twentieth century, e.g. Baldwin in the 1926 General Strike—and throughout the 1930s. Conservatives were prepared to accept *faits accomplis* (e.g. Welfare State institutions) and to sacrifice a good deal to the increasingly powerful Labour Movement—provided that conflict was avoided and the essentials of the existing system preserved.

Edward Heath's strategy failed: a negative growth rate, economic depression, and finally open confrontation: the negation of all he had stood for. The confrontation with the miners was, of course, lost—twice! As a result of this fatal error the election was lost and the Conservative Party rejected its leader: the era of 'Thatcherism' had begun.

Whether the 'new Conservatism' with its harder, more aggressive, economic policies, relying heavily on traditional *laissez-faire* economic theory will prove different in the long run to previous attempts at new initiatives in economic affairs, remains to be seen. If Sir Keith Joseph's monetarist policies are put into effect then the resultant unemployment will presumably provoke class conflict unprecedented in the twentieth century. Similarly, Mrs Thatcher's insistence on cutting public expenditure in the welfare field and on making people 'stand on their own feet' (*vide* her 1976 USA tour and TV broadcast) have to be tested against the realities of office before judgment is passed.

But, however tentative the conclusions, on the level of attitudes there does seem to be a retreat from the confident assertion of 'étatiste corporatism' as analysed by Harris[37] towards a more individualistic approach. Despite all the marked differences between 'managerial Conservatism' and 'aristocratic Toryism' many of the old attitudes remain and are perhaps more noticeable in the 1970s than they were in the 1960s or 1950s: the belief in order and hierarchy, the pessimistic interpretation of 'human nature' and thus the emphasis upon incentive on one hand and coercion on the other, and the pragmatic and flexible willingness to adapt to whatever circumstances prevail. Whilst the Disraelian concerns with national unity and Empire have left their mark, the emphasis of the Conservative 'Social Contract' has always been upon the functions and responsibilities of the governing class and the need for a strong but civilized élite,[38] rather than upon the rights and powers of the people in a universal suffrage political system. The fine balance of hard-headed self-interest and an ideologically reasonable rhetoric of justification has been carefully nurtured over the years: *and*, to add a further dimension, this has developed not through design but through a natural convergence of ideology, reality and rhetoric. Perhaps the Conservatives have a greater natural 'feel' for politics than everybody else . . .?

Yet this balance seems seriously out of key at present: the Conservative Party under Mrs Thatcher is undergoing a (temporary?) period of crisis. No longer can Conservative strategy be based upon economic growth, however modest. One short-term answer is to adopt the Labour Party's attempt at a social contract with organized labour: but the Conservatives have no such relationship, actually or potentially. (Although with the present divisive Trade Union movement the Party may well attempt an alignment with the 'craft' unions.) Another alternative appears to be being pursued by Mrs Thatcher's Conservative Party—to hark back to the middle-class, small business, quasi-nineteenth century Liberal rhetoric so beloved by the suburban South. Is this a genuine attempt to reverse the 'étatiste' trends of previous years? Can the Conservative Party be serious in its commitment to extricate the capitalist economic structure from State involvement? Even if the conservative strata in society generally support this somewhat romantic, nostalgic return to individualistic ideology, it is inconceivable that those who hold economic power, the owners and managers of British industry, would countenance this sort of move. Much more likely on past experience, is that this sort of rhetoric, albeit more extreme than in the past, will remain rhetoric and will either be ignored or even countered when the Conservatives return to power (as, for example, happened in the case of Resale Price Maintenance with Edward Heath). There is thus a crisis of *ideology*—with the party moving further and further from the interests and political aims of its ultimate power base: the managerial ruling class. In the present economic situation no industrialist would welcome a situation in which market forces are left to determine levels of economic activity! Visualize the Upper Clyde, Rolls Royce, or British Leyland without any government aid or involvement. The present economic structure—let alone the complex and carefully nurtured relations between the State and organized labour—would be unable to adapt to the sort of *laissez-faire* policies advocated by the Conservatives. Electorally, the present policies may well attract the hard-pressed middle-class voters, but the Conservative Party remains ultimately the Party of big business—and it must integrate itself with these interests if it is to survive.

In the concluding pages of his book Harris argues that the task facing the Conservative Party—to transform itself 'from a party of small and large national business to one of international companies' —is one of the major challenges in its history 'for it would involve the dissolution of the national British State on which the Conservatives have been for so long dependent.' The choice is 'internationalization or suicide'. Since this was written (1972) Britain has of course begun this process with entry into the EEC. It is significant though that Mrs Thatcher's Conservative Party gives far less emphasis to the importance of the EEC than did Mr Heath's. The whole emphasis has shifted on to the national, almost parochial, level. It remains to be seen whether Mrs Thatcher and the new Conservatives will be able to transcend this parochialism when they achieve power: the combination of national and international problems is indeed formidable. The phenomenon of multi-national industry plus the political institution of the EEC, added to the national but chronic problems of the British economy, challenge not only the short-term capacity of the Conservative Party, but the whole Conservative idea. To date the Party has shown little aptitude for marrying an adherence to the traditional, nationalist and élitist conservative values to the contemporary context of multi-national bureaucratic capitalism. Unless it can rediscover its old ability of adaptation to new circumstances we may see the end of the Conservative Party and with it the Conservative framework—to be replaced by the corporatist social democracy of the Labour Party.

As a postscript on Conservatism, it is worth looking, very briefly, at Conservative attitudes to welfare provision. This is obviously the area which impinges most overtly on social work and it is also an aspect of Conservatism that has been widely misunderstood, especially in recent years. The common assumption, at least on the Left, has been that Conservatives are, and always have been, opposed to welfare provision and that, as the party of the rich they have accepted 'Welfare Statism' grudgingly and without understanding. There is, to our mind, some truth in this, but like many generalizations, it is too simplistic. To begin with there has, from the beginnings of Toryism, been a tradition of aristocratic benevolence: part of the 'social duty' (referred to earlier) which Conservatives have always considered to be the corollary of their role as governors. (This benevolence was not of course wholly disinterested: the social control exercised *via* welfare provision throughout the ages has been invaluable for government and has formed an integral part of the apparatus of the State. As with Shaw's Mr Undershaft some believe that the Tories do the 'right' thing for the wrong reason!) This strain of *noblesse oblige* was immeasurably re-inforced by the advent of Disraelian Tory democracy with its emphasis upon social welfare.[39] However, in practice, as opposed to rhetoric, the Disraelian achievement was an extension of Conservative welfare thinking rather than a complete break with tradition: despite Disraeli's genuine concern with the social conditions of the poor there is little evidence that he had any idea of major State involvement in welfare provision. Moreover, as Samuel Beer notes,[40] Disraeli was determined that any innovations and improvements in social welfare provision should not lead to new taxes: a not unfamiliar proposition.

Nevertheless, the psycho-political advantages of insisting upon a concern with social welfare should not be underrated—not only as seen in Disraeli, but also in his more recent heirs such as Butler, Macmillan, Boyle and even Keith Joseph in his DHSS days. Combined with the traditional aristocratic concern, this makes for a strong ideological conviction in the Conservative Party that social welfare is an integral aspect of policy.

This whole ethos runs alongside the mainline 'managerial'

ideological trend within the party, which tends to view any expenditure on welfare as economically wasteful and politically undesirable. This latter trait has indeed been dominant, but it is important to realize that a commitment (and a strongly held commitment) to welfare provision also exists in certain sections of the Conservative Party.

Given this analysis it is not surprising that the twentieth century Conservative Party has not objected violently to individual acts of social welfare provision. What is perhaps more unexpected is the acceptance by the Conservative Party of the broad structure of the Welfare State since its inception in 1945. Not only was, and is, the Welfare State thought (erroneously)[41] to be redistributive in terms of wealth and access to social amenities, the Welfare State has in effect nationalized welfare and brought all major services under the central control of the bureaucratic institutional structure of the State.

However, just as the Party adapted to new conditions in the mid-nineteenth century, so the Party since 1945 has come to accept Welfare Statism as a socio-political fixture—a permanent part of the political furniture. With the realism which is one of their greatest assets, the Conservatives realize that there is no purpose—electoral or otherwise—in trying to dismantle the Welfare State. Characteristically, the Conservatives have reacted to external circumstances and accepted the social directions of change (where they do not threaten the kernel of the existing structure). Thus, the Party has been prepared to *accept* the drift towards State involvement but not anxious to *promote* these policies. In so far as the Party leadership has given conscious consideration to the general question of Welfare Statism it has tended to regard Welfare State provision as part of the price that has had to be paid to an increasingly powerful Labour Movement to keep the existing system viable.

Prior to 1945 the Conservatives had, of course, a very different emphasis from Labour on welfare policy. Whereas the Labour Movement was striving to achieve a national, all-embracing, State supported system of welfare provision,[42] the Conservatives—even the most welfare-oriented—held to the traditional view that welfare provision should be granted to the 'poor and needy' only. Historically it had been recognized by Tories that 'the poor are always with us': the task of enlightened Toryism was to cater for the welfare of this residual section of society, but not to create a total system of welfare provision. More than a little of the Victorian ethics of 'self-help' underlie twentieth-century Conservatives' attitudes to social welfare provision and this has resulted in policy terms in differences of emphasis even after 1945. (Perhaps the most important of these being the Conservatives' insistence upon the desirability of means-tested benefits, compared to Labour's policy of wholesale provision.)

After 1945 Conservatives have, as is so often the case, adapted to new circumstances and accepted the concept of the Welfare State. Through the Conservative governments of the 1950s and 1960s Conservatives occasionally attempted to cut back social provision in various fields—but, generally, policies have differed little from those of the Labour Party and there has certainly been no attempt to dismantle, or even restructure, the basic institutions of the Welfare State. However hostile Conservatives, locally as well as nationally, may have been to the ideology underlying Welfare State provision they have accepted political reality and contented themselves with, at most, minor reductions and rhetorical denunciations.

Moreover, and this final point is of extreme importance in the social work context, the Conservative Party has seen the operation of a centralized social service apparatus as an important means of social control: at the most cynical the Welfare State can be argued by Conservatives to be a useful means of neutralizing potential discontent with the social order and has certain regulative features which enable the Government to tighten the screws a little when necessary. Control of social welfare - poverty levels is indeed a powerful and frightening addition to the armoury of State power.

This fairly relaxed attitude to social policy questions operated through the 1950s and 1960s. By the 1970s growth-oriented Conservatism had given way, as we have argued, to a more *laissez-faire* attitude, opposed to State intervention in welfare as in all else. (It is important to emphasize again that Conservative opposition, such as it is, is to the Welfare State—the bureaucratization and State control—rather than the concept of welfare as such.) It remains to be seen whether this policy of cutting back, across the board and long term, will be put into operation; but if we are to believe Mrs Thatcher we may well see the next Conservative administration taking a major initiative in reducing State expenditure on welfare (but not on social control) agencies. If this proves to be the case, social policy could, for the first time since 1945, be one of the areas where the two ideological frameworks of Conservatism and social democracy are in serious conflict.

Marxist view of Conservatism[43]

The Conservative perspective on society is held, by Conservatives, to be based upon a coherent philosophy—composed of a coalition of perspectives and ideas gleaned from a variety of periods but forming a cohesive whole and constituting the justification for political action and social-political theorizing. At the kernel of all Conservative philosophy is the concept of the 'preservation of the *status quo*' (or more often, of the 'essentials' of the *status quo*), and this in itself is justified by reference to 'deeper continuities' in 'human nature' and in the 'British character'.

Yet industrial society is characterized by rapid and continuous change and Conservatives are able to offer no evidence of consistency in concepts such as 'British character'. As Harris points out Toryism did not suffer from this problem in the pre-industrial, fairly static society: 'Christian civilization was secured by the three elements, God, aristocracy, soul, retaining supremacy by the accepted subordination of Man, masses and passions.'[44] There is, Marxists claim, no validity in the Conservatives' claim to an unchanging philosophy: the party that has changed from support for 'the land' to support for 'entrepreneurial capitalism' and, again, from this to support for bureaucratic monopoly capitalism, can hardly claim total consistency.

Marxists would conclude with Harris, that[45]

> The party exists as a means of unifying the political opinions of different groups within the ruling class, of different élites, and giving them political expression . . . The political—as opposed to electoral—success of the party turns upon its ability to continue to recruit rising groups within society and represent them politically, at the same time resisting complete identification with declining groups.

The party provides a political outlet for the ruling élites that go to make up what, in Marxian terms, is precisely described as the ruling class.

The Conservatives' central purpose is thus to maintain order and power—to secure the survival of a ruling class. It is important here to note that the Conservative view is centred on a concern for the preservation and consolidation of *a* ruling class and not the *existing* ruling class. Conservatives have had a flexible attitude over almost everything except power. The main motivating force has been the maintenance of the organizational role of the party as the representative force of the dominant socio-economic power. More generally, Conservatives have held that the maintenance of social and political power in 'responsible' hands has been the primary objective of collective action. Thus definitions change from period to period, not only of what it is important to preserve but of who should be entrusted with that preservation. (As Harris notes,[46] 'The party of land did nothing to prevent the disastrous decline of British agriculture from 1870 to 1914. The party of business admitted a degree of State regulation that, to an earlier generation of businessmen, would have appeared indistinguishable from a socialist nightmare.')

Thus far the Marxist analysis of Conservatism, whether accepted or not, is at least clear: historically, the Conservative perspective generally, and the Conservative Party in particular, has stood for little except the maintenance of political power by means of a permanent alliance on continually shifting ideological ground, with the economically dominant groups in society. The presentation of 'continuity' and 'tradition', as 'Conservative philosophy' is so much window-dressing. Two things need emphasis here: first, this is not only a Marxist view—it is shared by a very large proportion of social democrats.[47] Second, this analytical view of the Conservative party relegates the supposed ideology to a point of no importance—but this is not to deny that, subjectively, the Conservative 'philosophy' is an essential component of Conservative thinking. It is a great mistake to dismiss the Conservative Party on conspiracy theory grounds: the Conservative Party, and the more general Conservative attitude, is not a hypocritical conspiracy of ruthless Dickensian exploiters who use the Conservative framework of ideas as an ideological mask to fool people deliberately. On the contrary, the strength of the Conservative Party lies to a great degree in its ability to convince not only its supporters but its leaders of the validity of its ideology.[48] Thus from a Marxist viewpoint, Conservatism is objectively a political expression of the ruling class at any given period: there will be 'time lags' between socio-economic and political changes within Conservatism (leading, for example, to the split in the nineteenth century between the 'landed Tory' and 'industrial Conservative' and in the twentieth century between 'liberal' and 'étatiste' views of Conservatism)—but, ultimately, Conservatism adapts to the interests and ideology of the dominant class. There can thus, by definition, be no continuity or coherence about Conservative ideology.

On the other hand, the extent to which, subjectively, Conservative ideology and rhetoric plays a crucial role in moulding together a coherent political ideology at any given time must not be underrated. One of the major aspects of the Conservative achievement has been the ability to translate socio-economic reality into political rhetoric and policy acceptable to its supporters *and*, usually, to link such new policy directions into the supposedly coherent, continuous tradition of Conservative philosophy.

In the light of this general conception of Conservatism what have Marxists to say of the contemporary Conservative perspective? All Marxists hold that because of the inbuilt contradictions of capitalism the political (as well as the economic and social) system is under increasing pressure. The Conservative Party as, fundamentally, the party of the ruling class is liable to ever greater stress. Moreover, given the preceding analysis which argued that the Conservative Party reacts to rather than creates or interacts with ideological (and socio-economic) change, the *pace* at which the Conservative Party has had to change since 1945 in order to keep abreast of 'modern trends' has been unprecedented.[49]

The conflict, so well described by Harris, between 'liberal Conservatives' and 'étatiste Conservatives' is not yet over. If Heath can be described as the apotheosis of 'étatiste Conservatism' then surely Mrs Thatcher marks a strident revival of the old *laissez-faire* spirit of entrepreneurial times.[50] In many ways Mrs Thatcher echoes nineteenth-century Liberalism with her stress upon individualism, lack of State involvement and so on. The Conservative Party is in a state of crisis, as we argued earlier. From a Marxist point of view this reflects both the political uncertainty of the Party and the ruling class: as economic and social crisis deepens in the Western capitalist world generally (and in Britain in particular) the Conservative Party is having to make more and more concessions. At the same time this very crisis has precipitated a change of orientation from the managerial and growth-dominated ideas of the 1950s and 1960s to the 'backwoodsmen' approach of Mrs Thatcher, and the Party is thus getting out of step with the ideas and interests of the major industrial and commercial concerns. Although constrained by economic and political conditions to abandon their consensus-oriented approach of the 1950s and 1960s the Party remains deeply committed to the existing structure of monopoly capitalism—and indeed dependent on both the personnel and institutional power of this structure for support, financial and political. Moreover, the Conservative Party is deeply imbued with the traditions of British parliamentarianism and has to a very great degree incorporated the ideology of nineteenth-century political Liberalism (at least in terms of its respect for 'democratic' institutions, and the fundamental political freedoms—of the press, of speech and so on).

The Conservative Party is thus a complex political structure—founded undoubtedly, Marxists would argue, on the maintenance of ruling-class power in the political sphere as in the economic—but with many overlapping and conflicting ideological trends operating within it. The development of the Conservative Party, and the national Conservative perspective, will depend upon the intra-party interaction between the various forces and the wider interaction between the party as a whole and the industrial and commercial complex.

From the Marxist point of view Conservatives are continually walking the tightrope between their objective and subjective roles. As the contradictions within capitalism become more acute so the role of ideology within Conservatism assumes an ever greater importance. Ultimately the ideological divide within Conservatism must be resolved. What direction this resolution will take depends upon socio-economic developments. If socio-economic crisis deepens Conservatives may well find it impossible to both maintain the kernel of the existing system (i.e. the power of capital) and adapt sufficiently to avoid serious social and political conflict. In the circumstances it is by no means inconceivable, Marxists argue, that the Conservative Party will transform itself into an authoritarian movement of the extreme Right—protecting capitalism by force rather than ideology.

Marxists have tended either to ignore or underrate the Conservative Party: in future they will do so at their peril. Only recently has any serious analytical attention been paid to the Party either historically or ideologically. This is a major failing and is indicative of an all too frequent arrogance and crudity in British Marxist writing: it has been assumed too often that the Conservative Party is composed of bucolic squires, corrupt businessmen and P. G. Wodehouse characters. The fact that the Conservative Party has been in power for more than forty of the seventy-seven years of the twentieth century is enough to show how serious a political force it is.

Chapter four

Political culture of contemporary Britain (2): social democracy

To pursue our examination of the political culture from which modern social work has evolved, we now turn to the remaining part of the ideological equation: the origins and development of social democracy (via Liberalism) which has strongly influenced the ethos and the practice of social work in Britain.

The Conservative view of things may be the most well established and deeply ingrained but since the mid-nineteenth century it has been those who have called for change and reform who have dominated social and political thinking. Indeed, the Conservative view of society since the mid-nineteenth century can be understood only if it is realized that in large part the Conservatives—both large and small 'c'—have been on the defensive and reacting to the social and political reforms advocated by others.

First Liberalism and later social democracy have been the positive forces in British politics in the nineteenth and twentieth centuries— initiating reform, refining ideology and dominating social and political life. The movements are, of course, different in a variety of ways—not least ideologically—but they have in common a positive, initiating and reformist perspective. As we have argued, the Conservative perspective is a hybrid with numerous attitudes overlapping and conflicting—but the modern social democratic movement is even more diverse in composition. To disentangle the jungle of social democratic ideology, two distinct and fundamental questions must be asked: subjectively, what do the various groupings within the social democratic framework believe about politics and society?; and, objectively, which group or groups hold power within social democracy and what social and political functions do these groups fulfil?

Before beginning this discussion we need, however, to clarify the

Political culture of contemporary Britain (2): social democracy

definitions of some of the terms: not only is the ideology of social democracy a jungle, the nomenclature of different ideological strains has varied confusingly from period to period. The two major frameworks we are discussing in this section are Liberalism and social democracy: the mainstream of reformist politics in Britain in the nineteenth and twentieth centuries. Liberalism, as an ideological perspective rather than a political party, is a nineteenth-century phenomenon and represents, as Raymond Williams notes,[1] 'the highest form of thought developed within bourgeois society'. It is based, at least as far as the nineteenth century is concerned, upon an individualistic ideology developed within the context of a capitalist society: it is therefore best characterized as a perspective of 'possessive individualism'. Theoretically, then, Liberalism is opposed not only to socialism but to any form of social perspective. All forms of socialism have in common a collectivist perspective of some sort and are, therefore, fundamentally at variance with the Liberals' individualism. However, in Britain, there are in fact many links between Liberalism and social democracy—historically and ideologically. This arises partly because, historically, the social democratic movement inherited, in a direct continuum, the reformist tradition of the Liberal movement of the nineteenth century, and partly because, ideologically, British social democracy derived its impetus not from the mainstream of European socialism, but from a peculiarly British amalgam of utilitarianism, Trade Union pragmatism, and Nonconformist radicalism. Social democracy can thus be characterized as fundamentally Liberal, in terms of its commitment to individual freedom, the parliamentary system and so on, and collectivist in its support of State involvement and control across a wide sector of social and economic life.

Our purpose here is to analyse the various aspects of the social democratic perspective both ideologically and historically. In order to do this the links between Liberalism and social democracy must also be explored. Liberalism will be discussed here, therefore, not for its own importance (which in the nineteenth century was absolutely paramount), but purely in the context of its influence upon the development of British social democracy.

One essential preliminary point when discussing the nature of British social democracy must be made. British 'Socialism' differs from all other European Labour movements, not only because it was the first to emerge, but, more importantly, because of a number of unique features in British political culture.[2] This is not the place to go into detail but we need to note that, following the English Civil War, the United Kingdom went through a period of consolidation when, through a partial unification of the monied and landed interests, a stable social base was established. Despite all the enormous social, economic and political changes of the nineteenth century, this sociologically stable society emerged, if not unscathed, at least basically intact. It is against this background of social and political stability that both Liberalism, and, later, social democracy must be measured. At the time, of course, this social stability was far less apparent and ruling circles were fearful of revolution.[3] There was a confusing and contradictory pattern in the early years of British working-class activity, with a Trade Union consciousness developing side by side with a close adherence to orthodox Liberal ideology.[4] Liberalism exerted an enormous influence on the crucial period of the Labour Movement's organizational beginning. Liberalism was a product of a very specific historical period characterized by early and rapidly expanding industrial capitalism. For a brief period of thirty to forty years the Liberal Party—and the overall Liberal ideology—dominated social and political life in Britain before the waters closed in around it after the First World War.[5]

In its early years the Liberal Party *was* the party of the new industrialism: founded on Benthamite principles[6] of *laissez-faire* individualism, it fulfilled precisely the rationale needed by both the commercial and industrial sections of the new capitalist class.

Early Liberalism saw the individual and his welfare as the key, both in theoretical and practical policy-making terms, to society. If the individual was able (and encouraged) to improve his own standard of living, then society as a whole would benefit through an amalgamated total of enlightened self-interest. To give maximum opportunity for these objectives to be achieved a strategy of social and political non-interference by government was essential. These *laissez-faire* principles applied not only to government non-interference in social legislation but in the economic and political spheres too. Thus Benthamite social theory links in closely with traditional classical economy which holds to the sanctity of the free market and the importance of allowing complete freedom for supply and demand to determine production levels, price and distribution, etc.; any interference with this natural mechanism distorts and thus makes inefficient the whole system. This philosophy of non-interference applied also to the international economic situation: it was argued that Free Trade would enable the most efficient concentration of production—and thus an overall rise in international levels of productivity and economic activity.

In this Liberal individualism the early industrialists found a rationale for untrammelled economic growth: not only was the unimpeded expansion of capitalist industry beneficial materially to the individual entrepreneur, it was also necessary for economic growth and the general welfare of society. The links with the Protestant ethic have often been noted[7] and we should stress here the

Political culture of contemporary Britain (2): social democracy

close interrelationship between the work ethic, the 'self-help' philosophy of the individualist creed, and the importance of Nonconformist religion as a basis of the nineteenth-century Liberal culture.[8]

The proposed role of government under this system was negligible: first, to administer a basic minimum of government affairs (especially foreign relations) and second, to widen the franchise to include the new rising industrial class and at the same time oppose the old ruling class of the landed aristocracy. Any greater involvement by government would distort the 'natural balance' and was therefore undesirable.

Liberals thus found themselves opposing any measures designed to alleviate the hardships of the early industrial system: there was, for example, strong opposition to Trade Unionism, to factory legislation and so on—the human suffering caused by the Poor Law Reform of 1834 (which was inspired by Benthamite principles) became a *cause célèbre* in the Labour Movement.

These policy implications of Liberalism ensured the full support of the entrepreneurial class in mid-Victorian Britain, but, paradoxically, the obvious and extreme cruelty of the results of the logic of Benthamism was at variance with the humanitarian strand within Liberalism. By the end of the century, thanks to the refinements of Utilitarianism (especially as seen in the work of J. S. Mill and T. H. Green) the Liberals had become convinced that freedom for the individual depended upon the quality of the environment: it was thus the duty of the government to ensure that conditions enabling genuine freedom of choice were created. The whole ethos of State non-interference was thus seriously eroded, and, whilst individual freedom remained the basis of Liberalism, the means of achieving this desired end had changed radically. With J. S. Mill the ideology of Liberalism brought theory into line with the practising politicians' ideas of short- and mid-term government legislation. *But* this radicalization of Liberalism divorced the Liberal party, irrevocably, from its class base amongst the entrepreneurial and related groups: support for Liberalism rapidly dwindled once it was realized that Liberals were likely to introduce social and economic reform which would restrict the freedom, and the profits, of the industrialists.

Even in the heyday of Liberalism then there was an inconsistency between a capitalist class base and an idealistic, progressive political party: the inherent radicalism of the Party was also at odds with the Party leadership's more cautious, conservative attitudes. Much of the radicalism was populist in inspiration and influenced by anti-Parliamentarist, Rousseauist ideas—throughout the nineteenth century Radicals were involved in extra-parliamentary movements and agitation.

With the extension of the suffrage and an increasing swing to the left within Liberalism, Radicalism became more and more integrated into the mainstream of Liberal politics. By the late nineteenth century Radicals had been absorbed into Liberalism or had split off into one of the (many) socialist societies. Ultimately, though, Radicalism with its insistence on democratic control and social reform, represented the most intellectually (and emotionally) cogent aspect of Liberalism and is of considerable importance in its influence upon the later social-democratic movement.

The third important strand within Liberalism was 'Nonconformism'. Many Liberals were motivated by religious and moral convictions and went into politics and social activity believing that through the individualist creed (and through creating an individualistic, thrifty, competitive, puritanical social structure) a qualitatively better society could emerge. In a very real sense Liberalism was seen as the political arm of a moral and religious crusade,[9] and had its 'grass roots' support in the Methodist chapels of the industrial North, Wales and Scotland. The parallels with social work development are striking. Many social workers are motivated by the Christian ethic in wanting to eradicate those elements and institutions in society which, they hold, are the root cause of so much misery and suffering, e.g. drink, gambling, sexual exploitation through commercialism, etc. Moreover, this perspective is couched within the wider assumptions of an individualistic way of seeing the world and bases its analysis and objectives on the assumption of treating 'individuals in trouble' (rather than seeing problems as socially created and therefore requiring socially based solutions). The Nonconformist tradition had its policy preoccupations which are well enough known (e.g. temperance movement, disestablishment and so on)—what is less often noted is the strong boost to the individualistic assumptions and arguments of Benthamism which this Christian tradition gave to Liberalism. The idea that politics was basically about the salvation of lost souls and the righting of obvious wrongs was a simple but powerful creed and became a deep influence on the Independent Labour Party in the late nineteenth and early twentieth centuries (see also pp. 48-50).

Liberalism was thus, from the beginning, a coalition of interests and theories, some of which were ultimately quite incompatible. This is not the place to go into the reasons for the decline of Liberalism[10] but the gradually widening gap in the perspectives of politicians (Radicals and others), Nonconformist working-class voters and the industrial interest, demonstrated the working through of these divisions. Once the party's entrepreneurial class base had deserted *en masse* to the Conservatives, and the Party had failed to exert itself to capture the new institutions of the organized Labour

Political culture of contemporary Britain (2): social democracy

Movement, the Liberals found themselves trapped in a political vacuum. By the turn of the century they were, in broad terms,[11] nearer agreement over policy than before but they were effectively without support from either the rich or the masses. With historical hindsight the famous 1906 government seems to be a rather chaotic swan-song and a prelude to a new and more troubled era. The historic role of the Liberal Party was to help create and service the free market economy of early capitalism *and* bring to birth the democratic environment and institutions that were to destroy it.[12]

What has the impact of Liberalism in its various forms been on the social democratic perspective in the twentieth century? The *alpha* and *omega* of the British Labour Movement—particularly in relation to political culture, i.e. to *perceived* political views—lies in the Trade Union movement. The 'Labour Movement' as an organized and self-conscious representation of the British working class had existed for eighty years before the Labour Representation Committee (the forerunner of the Labour Party) was created in 1900. The Labour Movement has thus always been, unlike the Conservative and Liberal Parties, a predominantly extra-parliamentary movement out of which the Labour Party developed. Thus, throughout the formative years of the Labour Movement—through the early years of Trade Unionism, Chartism and the rest—the Liberal ethos was dominant. What effects did this have? This is not the place to go into any detail about the historical development of the British Trade Union movement,[13] and from the point of view of political attitudes within social democracy in the twentieth century much of the early history of Trade Unionism is irrelevant. We do however need to identify the main ideological trends as it is through these that 'Labourism' developed. In many respects nineteenth-century Trade Union history can be seen as a continual battle between the ideologies of Left and Right, with the Right being generally, but not always, in the ascendancy. When Trade Unions began to develop in the 1820s and 1830s there were initial attempts at revolutionary industrial organizing of various types (e.g. the Grand National Consolidated Trades Union of Robert Owen)—all of which failed because of their administrative and political ineptitude, combined with an extraordinarily naïve optimism about the ease with which a new society could be created.

Partly as a reaction to these failures, and partly as a response to direct economic self-interest, new unions of skilled artisans with quite different objectives were established in the mid-nineteenth century. The characteristics and perspectives formulated during this period formed the basis of the ideological perspective of the organized Labour Movement from that time onwards. The core beliefs of the Trade Union movement stem from the 'New Model

Unions' of the 1850s—and much of the ideology, as well as the strength of the political Labour establishment—can be traced back to the same crucial period.[14]

The ideology of this 'New Model' group is thus of key importance in establishing the nature of British social democracy. The cornerstones of the 'New Model' perspective rested on the common sense, pragmatic assumption that Trade Unions were, primarily if not exclusively, in business to further the material interest and job security of their members. It followed from this that 'political' action to achieve radical change was not part of the Trade Unions' function: far from wanting to overthrow the existing social order the 'New Model' leaders accepted Liberal/Radical views of society and enthusiastically lent their support to the Liberal cause. Their concern as Trade Unionists, however, lay in the provision of immediate industrial benefits for their members: thus they were concerned with obtaining welfare benefits across a wide range (e.g. unemployment, sickness, funeral, etc.) and with preserving job security. Both these objectives are of key importance in determining future developments within the Labour Movement: the concern for material and 'pragmatic', tangible, benefits has dominated the Trade Union section of the Labour Party and many Trade Unionists think of the Labour Party's primary reason for existence as the advancement of working-class living standards. This is, of course, a profoundly ideological view of the role of Trade Unions and the Labour Party and has led to a deeply ingrained anti-socialist perspective.

Just as important is the divisive and widely held view within Trade Unions that the people at the bottom of the social pile—those who are inadequate in a whole variety of ways and who are the victims of our social and economic system—are no concern of the organized Labour Movement. Social workers will be all too familiar with the negative and narrowly self-interested perspective of the 'respectable working class'. This divisive, sectional consciousness originated in the early Trade Union structure where the emphasis was exclusively upon the protection of privileged status and the acquisition of material benefits. Social attitudes may have changed over the years in many respects but in terms of psycho-political perspectives there appears to be depressingly little change.[15]

Similarly, the concern of the 'New Model' Trade Unions with 'job security'—which stemmed in part from their role as representatives of the relatively small sections of skilled artisans—laid the basis for the almost obsessional concentration of British Trade Unionism upon differentials, and the resultant hierarchical structure, which has led, amongst other things, to a chronic lack of industrial unity. Far from the Trade Unions representing the will of a united working-class movement organized on a 'co-operative and fraternal' basis, it often seems as though the TUC acts as a forum for powerful rivals to sort out their differences and haggle over their proportion of the 'national cake'.

To achieve their 'moderate', 'non-political' aims the 'New Model' unions were determined to build upon a solid financial and administrative basis: high subscriptions were charged and, very soon, full-time administrators were employed. In order to prevent embezzlement, inefficiency and so on, complex democratic procedures were instituted to ensure that the Unions' officials operated under the control of their membership. As the Webbs[16] (and many others since) have demonstrated, this democracy was more apparent than real as financial affairs were tightly controlled from the central apparatus.

Within these seemingly straightforward administrative developments lie the roots of the subsequent Labourist structure: strong central control by a professional bureaucracy operating through a supposedly democratic party structure,[17] relating at different levels to the varying interests within the industrial hierarchy of Labour power.

On the wider political front 'New Model' leaders saw their role as one of pressurizing for the legalization of Trade Unions and the protection of Trade Union rights. (And, arguably, judging by the legislative programme between 1870 and 1884, the 'New Model' Trade Union objectives were largely achieved.) Apart from this activity, which anyway brought them into close contact ideologically and on a day-to-day basis with Liberal politicians, Trade Union leaders accepted lock, stock and barrel Liberal theories of economics and society. Through their Nonconformism the 'New Model' leaders found themselves in fundamental agreement with the Liberals over the Christian, moral and individualistic basis of political activity.

Their long-term objective—alongside the material and legislative improvements already mentioned—was to create a Trade Union movement that was generally thought to be 'respectable', 'moderate', 'responsible' and 'mature'—in short, a Trade Union movement that would be accepted as an integral and integrated part of the social and political structure. Again, far from setting themselves up in opposition to the existing system, the 'New Model' Trade Unions consciously set out to attain acceptance and integration. Through such a strategy they hoped to achieve a measure of political and industrial power to pursue their own 'sectional' interests. Given their undoubted success,[18] and their progressively apolitical stance it is not surprising that, in general, Trade Unions were hostile both to socialism and to the creation of a new independent, working-class political party. 'Politics' was not only complicated but irrelevant to

Trade Unions. Trade Unions should pursue their basic industrial aims irrespective of the overall social and political environment in which they found themselves. To indulge in political activity to change this environment could be not only dangerous and futile but counterproductive as it would lead to a rejection of Trade Unionism as 'revolutionary' by the ruling class. Added to this was the less easily definable but very real hostility to 'theory' which has characterized the British working-class movement from its inception to the present day. There has always been a deep-rooted pragmatism and a suspicion of 'idealistic', 'subversive', 'foreign' theory[19] and a belief in adapting practical short-term solutions to social and political problems. For good or ill the major emphases of the 'New Model' perspective were inherited by the political Labour Movement: the emphasis on pragmatism and the opposition to theory or indeed any long-term perspectives; a *de facto* acceptance of Liberal ideology[20] and a deep-seated hostility to socialism generally and Marxism in particular; an understanding of and empathy with the industrial working class and its complex and differentiated social structure; a concern with respectability—financial and social, as well as political; and, above all else, a transference of the short-term bargaining mentality of British Trade Unions to the political arena, and an implicit belief that the Labour Party really exists to gain security and material wealth for the working class. Although this describes Trade Union 'ideology' in the 1860s, the modernity of many of the assumptions is striking.

If the 'New Model' provided the pragmatic, conservative ideological backbone of British Labourism, the New Unions of the 1880s and 1890s—representing the unskilled workers of the booming industries (gas, transport, docks, engineering, etc.)—gave fire and drive to the movement which was attempting to create a new political force. It was due to the efforts of these 'New Unionists', and the Independent Labour Party that the LRC[21] was formed in 1900. The motivations of these 'New Unionists' were very different from the earlier skilled artisan organizations: unlike the 'New Model', the unskilled 'New Unionists' were at the bottom of the social pile and had no stake in the existing social order. They were much more inclined to combine industrial and political aims and objectives, using strike action both to secure short-term material improvement and long-term social change. Although many of the early leaders of 'New Unionism' were greatly influenced by the Marxist Social Democratic Federation,[22] the influence was superficial and short-lived. The real driving force behind the politics of New Unionism lay in the ILP. As Pelling has claimed,[23] the ILP was the major influence in the formation of the Labour Party—and, along with the ideology of the 'New Model' and the Fabians (see p. 50), forms the basis of the ideological amalgam that goes to make up the twentieth-century Labour Party.[24]

The ILP grew out of the New Union wave of the late nineteenth century and, although led largely by skilled men and *petit bourgeois* radicals, drew its mass support from the unskilled working class, principally in the Northern and Scottish industrial areas. The ILP's credo was a moral one: a partially secularized and politicized Nonconformism, heavily influenced by the Christian and Liberal traditions of individualism. Socialism was not, for the ILP, primarily an economic struggle (and certainly not to be conceived of in Marxist analytical terms): it was rather a moral crusade against an evil (and inefficient) system. Moreover, that system could be defeated, not as the Marxists said by mobilizing a class, but by the conversion (salvation) of individual men. Only by instilling the socialist moral code could socialism hope to triumph. In effect, the ILP inverted Marx and held to the belief that men's beliefs changed their environment: they were thus, in both the philosophical and the popular sense, idealists.

What constituted the socialist moral code which the ILP preached? Again, the kernel of the answer lies with Nonconformism—with the implantation of a 'sermon on the mount' Christian spirit to social and political relations.[25] Love was thus at the heart of the ILP creed and the pacific, egalitarian strain within Christianity was always at the forefront of ILP thinking. (Hence the large number of ILP members who opposed the First World War on moral/pacifist, rather than socialist, grounds.) Given this orientation, plus a somewhat naïve optimism, leading to the adoption of a Liberal, Utopian ideological framework,[26] it is hardly surprising that the ILP tradition in the Labour Party was at once both radical and strongly anti-Marxist.[27] The ILP thus inherited the perspective of the nineteenth-century Radicals and transformed this, *via* the working-class movement in the Trade Unions, into a socialism with a fundamentally moral base. The ILP beliefs were certainly simple (and, some would say, simplistic) and they envisaged few structural problems in achieving their social and political aims. After all, socialism was so obviously the *sensible* as well as the *good* solution . . . . . .[28] If private property had produced not only misery, degradation and poverty, but economic chaos and social conflict, then, the argument ran, surely men of good will (or indeed men of enlightened self-interest) could agree on the adoption of a new creed, where co-operation replaced competition; fellowship, conflict; equality, hierarchy; where, in short, 'good' socialism replaced 'evil' capitalism. The somewhat optimistic assumption that everyone (or almost everyone—the capitalists were regarded by most members of the ILP as villains of pantomime proportions) would accept the rightness of the socialist argument through persuasion and not class conflict, was deeply held and again shows the ILP's strong ideological links with Liberalism. In particular, in this context, it is important to note the ILP's implicit acceptance of the consensus model of politics. Not only did the ILP accept the parliamentary structure and believe that, through universal suffrage and a strong working-class movement, the existing institutions could be transformed, peacefully, into a co-operative socialist system; it also accepted the Liberal assumption of rationality; that is, the ILP believed that there is always one rational, correct solution for any social or political problem. If people would only listen to reason then consensus could be reached by men of goodwill. Socialism, being in the eyes of the ILP the rational solution, would thus evolve through argument, persuasion and education. This perspective underlies the whole evolutionary approach to socialism and is, of course, the antithesis of the class conflict analysis of Marxism.

The ILP represented the working-class, activist strain within the Labour Party—and for the first 18 years of the Party's existence virtually controlled the movement. It is the ILP (and the later ginger groups in the ILP tradition—'Victory for Socialism', 'Tribune Group', etc.) who have been the left-wing activists within the Party, continually trying to push Labour into socialist policies. *But*, and this is the crucial point, this radicalism was, and is, constrained within the ILP ideology already outlined: the radicalism thus consists, in the contemporary context for example, in the pressure to maintain and extend public expenditure and to safeguard working-class living standards. There is no wider perspective about the structure of capitalism, the causes of the crisis and a working-out of policy alternatives from this theoretical position: the ILP tradition is thus imbued (whether it is seen as a blessing or as a curse) with the **pragmatism so characteristic of British political culture as a whole.**[29]

These two strains—the 'New Model' and the 'New Union' - ILP—thus fused, somewhat unwillingly and with a wealth of compromise and bargaining,[30] to form the LRC in 1900. In broad, organizational terms, the Trade Unions provided the finance, the numbers and the organization and the ILP the activists, the convictions, the leaders, and the 'soul'. But there was a third element which in many ways became more important ideologically than these two: Fabianism.[31] In almost all respects Fabianism differed from other strains within the Labour Movement—indeed for a considerable time the Fabians refused to ally themselves with the LRC preferring instead to adopt a policy of 'permeation' of all political parties. The Fabian Society, founded in 1884, was small, wholly middle-class and London based. It had no Trade Union connections and little link with the wider

Political culture of contemporary Britain (2): social democracy

national and international movement. It was characterized by intellectual discussion—initially attempting to refute Marxian ideas of economics and later developing a post-Utilitarian pragmatism which became interwoven into a strong, coherent 'State Socialist' ideology.

Neither the personalities nor the history of the Fabian movement need detain us here[32]—in this context we need to discuss two issues: the context of Fabian ideology and its importance in the thinking and development of the British Labour Movement.

The Fabians' socialism derived from Utilitarianism—the State being substituted for the magic forces of *laissez-faire* of traditional Liberal theory. The keynote of Fabian ideology lies in the concept of a centrally planned and controlled State operating a publicly owned industrial system. Socialism is conceived as a rational, ordered alternative to the chaos of capitalism. To this extent perhaps they shared with all other socialists (Marxists, ILP, and others) a conviction that socialism would enable the rationality of economic and social planning for the common good, to replace the anarchy of capitalist development governed entirely by motives of private gain. But, whereas the ILP and the Trade Union strains of the Labour Movement (and for that matter the Marxists) emphasized the democratic role of the working class within the transition to socialism—and based their whole rationale on the working class taking power in the future socialist society—the Fabians actively opposed the idea of working-class control and mass-participatory democracy. Control must rest with 'experts'[33] if socialism was to achieve efficiency—to allow democratic control and participation was anathema to Fabians. The working class were an alien mass who did not understand the complexities of modern society—economically, politically, socially or in any other way. Socialism thus consisted in substituting for the capitalist class an élite of disinterested experts to control the new socialist society. Not only would this new ruling élite be capable of governing in the interest of the whole society (and not just a section of it) it would also be motivated by the ideas of social service, rather than money or power-seeking, and would be subject to control, via the parliamentary system, by the people.

Fabians thus envisaged the collectivist equivalent of the old paternalist social system—with the Fabian élite replacing the old aristocracy in its paternalistic care for the mass of the people. Coupled with this centralized collectivism went a meritocratic approach: the envisaged élite was not to be self-selecting or born into power—under the Fabian scheme social mobility would be extended to the utmost to enable the most able, from whatever social class, to rise into the élite.[34] The justification for the whole Fabian framework rested upon the criterion of efficiency: a collectivist and centralized economic system and a meritocratically governed selection mechanism.

The Fabian view of society (especially in the crucial period for Labour ideology from 1900-18) held that all traditional varieties of socialism laid too much emphasis on 'man as producer' (and thus on Trade Unions) and too little on 'man as consumer' (and thus too little on consumer and social planning). Whilst Trade Unions would be necessary to protect the working class in a socialist society, the main burden of control would rest with the consumer-oriented government.[35] Indeed, the whole of society was viewed by the Webbs and other Fabians in this light:[36]

> The Webbs pictured the nation as a family which in future would be headed by a benign service state, the first function of which, as in all families, would be to see that all are fed, clothed and housed. Then the more important aspects of national life, the spiritual and intellectual heritage, could be cultivated and disseminated. All this would be possible only if the state took on the character of a gigantic cooperative society, which would become less and less coercive the more it engaged in the tasks of 'national housekeeping'. Social conflict would not disappear, since producer-consumer antagonism would remain. But disputes would be resolved in an atmosphere of consensus, based on a generally-accepted notion of higher purpose in social life.

Fabianism thus posited a situation where *class* conflict would not arise (and where all conflict would significantly decrease because of the rational control by government). The secret of the consensus society, and thus of the efficiency-oriented socialist society, therefore lay in the hands of the twentieth-century Platonic Guardians. One need hardly add that these paragons of intellectual virtue bore an uncanny resemblance to the Fabians themselves!

If consensus were to be achieved then social change must be both effective and gradual. As the Webbs denied the Marxist analysis with its emphasis on class conflict, there should, again, be no long-term problem in changing social institutions and procedures to a more rational pattern. This progress could be achieved though only by a gradual process of convincing people and organizations of the need for such change. (This again involves the classic Liberal rationality argument—see pp. 23-4.) Evolution as a method, and effective practical social change as a means, were therefore integral to the operation of Fabianism.

Even such a harsh critic as Tom Nairn[37] concedes that

> The Fabians were the technicians of reform—perhaps the most

able reformers of this kind produced by socialism in any country. Their effort was always concentrated upon what was immediately practical; their acute sense of the possible, their great respect for the facts that concerned them, their armoury of information and argument, all these things made them *effective* reformers.

The Fabians were indeed incorrigible producers of blueprints for practical social policy reforms,[38] many of which were implemented and almost all of which showed a practicality and thoroughness which was noticeably lacking in the more emotionally couched policy statements of the ILP (and later the Labour Party itself). It was this 'gas and water socialism' approach which gave the Fabians credibility with the Trade Union movement: living proof that the middle-class intellectuals could deliver the goods in a way that the activist and—in establishment Trade Union eyes—socialist tainted ILP could not.

So much for the policy orientation of the Fabians and the ideology from which it sprang. If the Fabians had remained a relatively small and uninfluential group their ideas would have been of minimal interest—worthy of a footnote to the history of socialism.[39] In the event it has been the Fabians who have provided the overwhelmingly preponderant part of the Labour leadership's ideology. The history of the Labour Party since 1918 can be summarized in both organizational and ideological terms as a combination of Trade Union power and Fabian ideology. As with the early Labour Party the Trade Unions continued to provide the finance, organization, numbers and thus power in the Labour Party—but from 1918 the ideology of the leadership was increasingly Fabian in tone.

How did this come about? The most important development in these crucial years lay outside the Labour Party: the increasing collectivization of social institutions, partly because of the War[40] but largely as a result of the changing industrial structure, led to a massively increased role for the State. From 1916 onwards the State became the key factor not only in political and social policy, but in industrial and economic affairs too. This centralization of power, and the consequent bureaucratization of both industrial and political life, occurred quite independently of any Fabian initiatives but, in many ways, conformed (or could be made to seem as though it were conforming) to the Fabian blueprint for future social and political development. In short, things were moving the Fabians' way in the second decade of the twentieth century.

More specifically, the 1914-18 period saw a closer liaison between the Trade Union leadership and the Fabians. The very size of the Trade Unions gave them an economic, political (and, of course, industrial) importance far greater than they had enjoyed in the nineteenth century.[41] Moreover, the Trade Unions had, during the War, played a vital and central role with the Lloyd George government in organizing and controlling the domestic war effort.[42] This had given the Labour leadership the taste for power and reinforced their already strong belief that there was potential for social and political change in the interests of the working class. At the same time, the demise of old-style Liberalism, and the rise of a corporatist government structure under Lloyd George had both enhanced the importance of the Trade Union movement *and* caused a political vacuum on the reformist wing of British politics.

The time was thus ripe for the Labour Party to assume the role of a national party, distinct from the Liberals and able and willing to challenge for political power. In order to accomplish this major change—from a pressure group in Parliament to a major national party challenging for political office—it was essential that the Party had a clear, distinctive and unifying ideology. If the Labour Party were to become the identifiable, independent and conscious political expression of the working class, then it had to have a clearly recognizable and independent programme and image. In Arthur Henderson's words, 'some sort of socialist faith was the necessary basis for the consolidation of the Labour Party into an effective national force.'[43] Moreover, the Fabians had made the Labour Party both more respectable and more practical: not only had the Fabians the administrative skills and the pragmatic perspective referred to above, they also had even more importantly transformed the very concept of Socialism, and in the process made it far more acceptable to the Trade Union (and Labour Party) leadership.

Whereas the ILP had a deep belief in democratic control in all spheres[44]—and were thus ideologically sympathetic to the spirit of workers' control and syndicalist agitation which swept the country between 1909 and 1914[45]—the Trade Union leadership had rejected entirely moves towards workers' control in industry. Not only did this offend their 'conservative' ideology with its inbuilt hostility to socialism (or any form of sudden change), it threatened their own position of power which depended crucially upon the centralized and bureaucratic structure of Trade Unionism.

The Fabians' conception of the central tenet of socialism—the abolition of private property and the substitution of common ownership—was quite different. Capitalism was criticized not because it was evil—the evil effects were in fact by-products of a fundamental irrationality. Only by substituting a centrally-controlled national system organized along the lines already discussed, could these problems be overcome. 'Workers' control', and indeed any form of serious democratic participation, was thus a total anathema to the Fabians: the mass had to be 'guided' by an élite more experienced and more intelligent and therefore more efficient. The justification for nationalization was thus efficiency (because it enabled national centralized planning to operate) and not democracy.

The power structure, and to a large extent the ideology—they are of course interdependent—of the modern Labour Party was determined by this fusion, in 1918, of Fabian ideology and Trade Union power and political ambition. The issues of 1918 are fundamentally the same as have confronted the Labour Party since 1945—and continue to confront it in the 1970s.

The 'Right' has dominated the Party both at parliamentary and at national conference level as a result of the 1918 structure which gave virtual monopoly power to the Trade Unions at the expense, primarily, of the ILP.[46] Not only was the ILP manoeuvred out of power nationally, the creation of Labour Party constituency branches meant that individuals could now join the Party directly and not only through one of the affiliated societies (which, in practice, had usually meant the ILP). The ILP's links with the grass roots in the localities—the lifeline of its claim to represent the rank and file—was thus destroyed. Moreover, the Labour Party developed its own powerful, centrally organized and controlled bureaucracy, firmly under the command of the Fabian-dominated leadership.

Organizationally, then, the coming into being of the modern Labour Party in 1918 saw the eclipse of the ILP as a serious political force and the start of the permanent domination of the Party by the Fabian - Trade Union alliance. Since 1918 the original concept of the Labour Party as a democratically controlled organization subject to Annual Conference decisions has become increasingly unrelated to fact. On the few occasions when Conference has rejected PLP policy (e.g. the 1960 Unilateralist debate), conference decisions have been invariably and crudely overruled by the leadership.[47] There were enormous psychological advantages accruing to the Fabians because of their educated, sophisticated, articulate and generally middle-class style compared to the working-class ILP. The inbuilt tendency of the self-confident, and often able, middle-class radical to dominate working-class organizations is a common enough feature in a whole range of social and political activities (e.g. community action groups, parent-teacher associations) and its importance in the context of Fabian/ILP relationships should not be underrated.

Ideologically, 1918 was crucial as it saw the Labour Party committed for the first time to a socialist constitution. The adoption of the famous Clause IV—to 'secure for the workers by hand or by brain the full fruits of their industry and the most equitable distribution thereof that may be possible, upon the basis of the common ownership of the means of production (distribution and exchange, added in 1929), and the best obtainable system of popular administration and control of each industry or service'—appeared to the ILP to commit the Party to socialism in the sense of the abolition of private property and the *substitution of a democratic system of workers' control.*

The Fabians, of course, regarded the purpose of nationalization as centralized control and interpreted Clause IV in this light. With hindsight, and given the Trade Union and Fabian domination of the Party, it is not difficult to see why the Fabian interpretation became so totally triumphant.[48] But this confusion over Clause IV—with the ILP and their successors convinced that workers' control was enshrined within the constitution—persisted right through until the first majority Labour government was elected in 1945. And indeed beyond: even in the Labour governments of 1964-70 Clause IV was held up by the Left as a demonstration of the socialist (in the ILP sense) commitment of the Party.

The great advantage, as far as the Labour leadership was concerned, of this ambiguity over Clause IV was the ability to keep the Party united and on a firmly centrist or right-wing path. Given the increasingly 'anti-ILP' perspective and policies adopted by the Party throughout the 1920s and 1930s, there was a remarkable maintenance of Party unity and lack of serious and organized criticism.[49]

Webb had thus delivered the organization and the ideology of the Labour Party into the hands of the Fabians, albeit in favourable circumstances. It must be borne in mind, of course, that the Trade Unions held (and continue to hold) the ultimate organizational and financial power with the Party.[50] But, since 1918, the power axis of the Labour Party has been forged in an alliance between the Trade Union leadership and the PLP leadership, which in turn has been almost totally dominated by the Fabian 'right wing'. (There have, of course, been leftists within the hierarchy of the Party but, *without exception*, they have found either that left policies are 'impractical' in the Realpolitik world, or they have simply shifted to the Right. This is an important point in the 'legitimation' debate, see below, Chapter 6). Through this alliance the Right has maintained control over both Conference and PLP—and thus over the movement as a whole.[51] (And, of course, the Right-wing policies have resulted in solid electoral performances.)

Labour and New Social Order, the manifesto issued by the Labour Party in 1918 was, again, prepared by Sidney Webb. It was an ambitious document and committed the Labour Party to a wider, more cohesive, programme of reform than ever before. The contents[52] were couched in radical rhetoric and, although, as Miliband points out, the implementation of the manifesto could have made considerable alterations to the capitalist structure of society, it was by no means as socialistic in its implications as was thought at the time.[53] The significant point, however, is the cohesive, independent and socialist image which the manifesto gave to the Labour Party. From this time the Labour Party was committed to policies of socially oriented collectivism: social ownership of industry combined with a commitment to the development of a 'Welfare State' system.

What were the results of this post-war perspective when the Labour Party came to exercise real political power for the first time in 1945?[54] Again, this is not the place for a full discussion and analysis of the 1945-51 government's record:[55] the significant point is to 'test' the perspective formulated in 1918 against the actual performance of 1945-51 (and 1964-70) when Labour were in power.

A key indication of the Labour Party's interpretation of its socialist purpose has been its attitude to Clause IV. Socialism, of any variety, must be concerned in the long term with the abolition of an economic and social system based upon competition, the profit motive, and private property. The Labour Party since 1918 has been committed to a long-term policy of common ownership which would replace the existing economic structure: this has been seen by generations of socialists as the basis upon which the socialist society will be built—a necessary, but by no means sufficient, condition for socialism. This belief applied as much to the Fabian Right as to the ILP Left (or at least up until the 1950s)[56] even though, as we have already argued, their conceptions of the nature and purpose of common ownership were very different.

We do not need here to go into the details of the 1945-51 government's record: the relevance here is that, by 1948, the government had clearly enacted all the nationalization legislation that it thought necessary (with the exception of Steel). The industries that had been brought into public ownership (significantly, the phrase *common* ownership was being replaced by either *public* ownership or nationalization—both of which carried heavy Fabian overtones of centralization and bureaucratic control) were either public utilities or vital but declining industries.[57] The only exceptions to this were Road Transport and Steel—and these were the only measures that were opposed by the Conservative opposition. There was no intention of taking into public ownership 'the commanding heights of the economy'. At most, nationalization was thought of as enabling the government to plan more efficiently: some measure of Fabian ideas of a centrally controlled, efficient economy thus remained, but in a very half-hearted form. There was no question of using nationalization as a basis for the transformation of a capitalist economy to a socialist one—similarly there was outright hostility to any suggestion that nationalization should be construed as part of a democratization process in industry: there was little, if any, increase in workers' participation (let alone control) in those industries which were taken into public ownership.[58]

By the 1970s with the partial resurgence of the Labour Left the Party resurrected their nationalization proposals—and not only for the (numerous) ailing industries. Those on the Labour Left saw great hopes in the National Enterprises Board proposals: through this machinery it might be possible—gradually and avoiding confrontation—for the State to gain control of a substantial proportion of British industry. Many on the Left were sceptical of such plans but the proposals appeared to link the 'Fabians' and the 'Left' in support of 'progressive' policies. Again, however, the leadership had no intention of significantly changing the balance of economic power: opposition from financial and commercial sectors enabled Harold Wilson to moderate the NEB proposals on the grounds that international reaction to such measures would seriously damage the British economy.

Common ownership remains the stated objective of the Labour Party but hardly anyone believes that this is any longer a policy aim. Thus the central concept of socialism (of all types) having undergone a Fabian bureaucratization has now virtually disappeared from the political agenda.

In terms of attitudes the other major feature of 1945-51 (and indeed of the post-War period generally) has been the development of the so-called 'Welfare State'. Between 1945 and 1951 the process begun in the nineteenth century and advanced considerably by Lloyd George (and to an extent Neville Chamberlain), became firmly established: the institutionalization, through State agencies, of a wide variety of social welfare services.[59] Again, we are not concerned here with the details of the legislation but with the attitudes underlying the Welfare State.[60] Humanitarian concern for the working class in particular, but also for the needy in general, had long been a major concern of the Labour Movement,[61] and, with the experience of the 1930s behind them, a socialized and comprehensive system of welfare provision was an agreed priority for the Labour government of 1945.

This was indeed a policy objective shared by all sections of the Labour Movement: by the Trade Unions because of their obvious concern with the welfare of their members (and because of the pragmatic appeal of welfare legislation); by the Labour ('ILP') Left because of its historical and deeply-felt concern with the poverty and misery which they regarded as being a by-product of capitalism; and by the Fabians as part of a humanitarian, centrally-controlled and organized system of welfare provision paralleling the proposed economic central control. The Marxist Left have severe reservations about the Welfare State (see pp. 64-5). But for the majority of those active in the Labour Movement the Welfare State is an integral part of a humane, caring and civilized society. The emphasis in the 1950s and 1960s has been upon the preservation and extension of welfare services as a major part of the Labour Party's commitment to an improved 'quality of life' for ordinary people. This has been an increasingly pragmatic policy aim, divorced from wider questions of achieving structural change in order to bring about a socialist society. In this sense although Labour regards the creation of the Welfare State as one of its most significant socialist achievements, it is, arguably, indicative of the Party's drift away from any serious concern with structural socialist change.

What then are the major components of the contemporary perspective of the British Labour Movement? What, in fact, do British social democrats believe in and what do they hope for socially and politically from the future?

Unlike almost all other Western European nations[62] whose social democratic traditions developed as a direct result of revisions of Marxism, British socialism developed from its Trade Union movement and its radical Nonconformist roots.[63] To this was added the ideology of a collectivist, post-utilitarian socialism which exercised influence far in excess of its 'power-base'. This ideological coalition has, of course, adapted to differing conditions and its perspective has altered accordingly. No longer is *any* of the blueprints for socialism—whether Left, Right or Centre—held with such conviction and enthusiasm as was the case in 1955 (let alone 1945 or 1915!). In many ways social democracy, in the form of the Labour Party, has been on the retreat as a vehicle for socialist change[64] since its inception: undeniably, it has lost much of the Fabian inspiration for evolutionary socialism which characterized not only 1918 and the whole Webbian movement, but also the Crosland-Gaitskell revisionism of Fabian ideology in the 1950s.[65]

Since 1964 the Labour Party has been the dominant political force in Britain but has used this power not to create an alternative to capitalism but to adapt the Labour Movement to an acceptance of the existing system. The point here is not that the Labour Party has adopted a 'right-wing' version of socialism—it has had a Fabian concept of socialism since 1918—but that it has to all intents and purposes abandoned *any* commitment to a socialist perspective of *any* description.

There are, however, significant and noticeable respects in which the original coalition of attitudes within social democracy persists. The humanitarianism so characteristic of the 'ILP' strain within the Labour Movement remains: the fierce attachment to the social welfare perspective is apparent particularly on the Left, and in the late-1970s finds its expression for example in the widespread campaign against public expenditure cuts. The intensity of feeling on such issues is combined with a characteristic lack of analysis: throughout its history the Labour Left has had no theory to explain capitalism or to project the sort of socialist policies for which it was emotionally ready.[66] The crises and catastrophes of capitalism have thus come like curses from the gods—and the reaction has been to defend what social and welfare rights the working class has attained and *to give support to leadership campaigns to 'save the nation'*, to adopt the Dunkirk spirit of co-operative patriotic endeavour, and so on. The humanitarian spirit, coupled with a bewildered misunderstanding of the workings of the system, and a consequent inability to formulate coherent socialist alternatives, bedevils the left of the Labour Party in the 1970s as it has done since 1900 and before. There is, in the 1970s, much frustration on the Labour Left but little idea of how to remedy things long-term.

The weakening of the idealistic commitment of the Left is perhaps not quite matched on the right of the Labour Party—but amongst the Fabian wing of the party there has been widespread disillusionment over the comparative failure of centralized planning. More importantly, the advance of State involvement with industry, and of corporatist development in economic and social planning between government, industry and Trade Unions,[67] resulted in a quasi-State Capitalist system. This system, with its attendant social welfare policies appealed to many Fabians as indicative of the coming into being of a post-capitalist situation.

Having said this, there remains, of course, within the Labour leadership (and the Trade Union leadership), a deep-rooted belief in planning—national, State, central planning of the economy in the interests not only of efficiency but of society as a whole: by this planning mechanism, it is argued, an appropriate proportion of national wealth can be set aside for welfare and other socially desirable purposes.

Social democracy then does have a perspective of change: based on moral and emotional arguments is the belief that society *ought* to 'be better', to 'care more' and so on. Equally strong is the belief that 'planning' and 'consultation' are better tools to run industry than 'competition' and 'managerialism'. These are, though, isolated beliefs and not part of any coherent philosophy: hence the acceptance of concepts of 'national interest', 'income restraint', and so on. It is a far cry from the days of 1900 and 1918—and yet the same traditions and structures underlie the party and the wider social democratic movement. Reformist socialism has not worked (some would claim that it has never been tried): and thus the Fabians and the 'ILP' Left have lost the self-confidence they once had. The Trade Unions, where power has increased tremendously since 1945, maintain their pragmatic stance and accept the existing multinational capitalism and the corporate bargaining situation, with the same degree of 'tolerance' and apolitical stoicism with which they accepted the Liberal hegemony of the 1860s.

The Labour Party is thus a powerful Party representing powerful interests—it may well be for the moment at any rate the *most* powerful party representing the *most* widely-held perspectives of society—but with its present structure and ideology it can in no way claim to represent a socialist perspective. The crucial question, therefore, is whether Ralph Miliband is right when he claims that there is no hope of its being transformed into a party[68]

> seriously concerned with socialist change . . . they [the leaders] will see to it that the Labour Party remains, in practice, what it has always been—a party of modest social reform in a capitalist system within whose confines it is ever more firmly and by now irrevocably rooted.

Marxist view of social democracy

Marxists have, as we argued earlier, paid far too little attention to the analysis of British Conservatism. The same criticism cannot be made of Marxist analysis of the British Labour Movement! The vigour, consistency and sheer volume of Marxist criticism of 'Labourism' testifies both to the significance and the detestation attached to 'Labourism' by British Marxists.[69] Indeed, it is hard to find any reputable historical or theoretical defence of British 'Labourism' from a social democratic point of view. The volume and intensity of this criticism is hardly surprising given the central role which the organized Labour Movement plays within Marxist theory and practice. All Marxists[70] accept that the organized working class is the vehicle for socialist change (at least within Western society) whether that change is to come through revolutionary action or electoral politics (as, for example, in the politics of the British, Italian and French Communist Parties).

Moreover, all Marxists also agree that the pressures and contradictions inherent within the capitalist system will create tensions that result in increasing class conflict. This, in turn, creates the possibility of building a more militant and politically conscious Labour Movement. Given the appropriate 'subjective' conditions, the 'objective' mechanism of the system will arguably produce a polarization of positions which will form the basis for the social and political struggle from which socialism will emerge.[71]

In the light of this sort of schema the analysis of the role of the Labour Movement is obviously crucial for Marxism. Given the objective conditions for a socialist transformation (which, Marxists argue, have existed within the capitalist world for at least sixty or seventy years) why is it that the British Labour Movement has been dominated by an increasingly unsocialist and anti-Marxist ideology?[72]

A large part of the answer to this problem lies in the historical roots of the Labour Movement (see pp. 45-57). Yet even given these 'conservative', 'unsocialist' foundations, surely, according to Marxism, the traumas of 1926, the Depression, and the successive Labour governments since 1945, should have produced a polarization of political forces, and a realization on the part of the Labour Movement that only through a militant Communist-oriented Labour party could significant change come about.

The fundamental explanation offered by Marxists increasingly centres on the mechanisms by which capitalism has both adapted to changed circumstances in the twentieth century and constructed ways of 'legitimating' the existing social order through a whole range of State and quasi-State institutions. The debate over 'legitimation' is examined in Chapter 6 and in many ways represents the crucial dispute between Marxists and social democrats over both the nature of existing society and the possible methods of change. The failure of Western European Labour Movements to fulfil the expectations engendered by Marxist analysis can only be explained, in Marxist terms, by the concept of 'false consciousness' (i.e. the working class failing to realize its true interests and organize to defeat capitalism) which, in turn, relies upon the analysis of socialization, particularly institutional, quasi-State socialization, in twentieth-century capitalist society. These issues are discussed in detail in Chapter 6, but there is a range of 'secondary' issues relating to these general themes but concerned specifically with the nature of the Labour Movement which it is appropriate to discuss here. Many of the specific ideological and structural components of the Labour Movement reinforced the extraordinarily strong pressures on social democracy to conform to the existing social structure rather than oppose it.

The ideological domination of the Fabians within the Labour party, which was based upon a coherent, well-articulated conception of bureaucratic socialism, was opposed by a structurally weak and ideologically confused and unsophisticated Left. This basis of ideological domination was reinforced by an organizational structure which gave virtually total power to the Trade Unions and the right-wing leadership, and the Right has slowly but surely cemented

Political culture of contemporary Britain (2): social democracy

its hold over the party.[73] Yet it is the weakness of the Left as much as the strength of the Right which has led to this situation.

The intellectual and organizational failings of the early ILP have already been discussed (see pp. 48-50). But the same problem re-emerged in somewhat different form,[74] in the Bevanite period (and, somewhat less dramatically, in the 'Tony Benn situation' in the early 1970s). In the case of Bevan, an acknowledged leader of the Labour Left of the old ILP tradition and a superbly charismatic figure, the choice after twenty years of protest, lay in 1945 between taking office and creating a major institutional part of the Welfare State[75] and accepting collective responsibility for some most unsocialist (to his mind) policies, or maintaining his socialist purity and mounting an attack on Labourism from the Left. Put in these terms there was no choice and Bevan accepted office; by the late 1950s he had so far compromised his socialism that he was able to denounce publicly, forcefully, and to great effect, his erstwhile comrades on the unilateralist (CND) issue.[76] This example—which could be multiplied a hundredfold—highlights the dilemma for any Marxist, or even Left ILP Socialist such as Bevan, who wishes to be active politically in Britain. At the local and 'lower' level should the activist join the Labour party because it is, undeniably, *the* vehicle of working-class politics and therefore the central focus for socialist activity, or should the attempt be made to create an alternative, genuinely socialist political party committed to Marxist politics and explicitly oriented to the revolutionary rather than the parliamentary tradition? (For the radical social worker a similar dilemma arises: does he encourage community action via 'established' channels or should he attempt to create a political organization outside existing structures, in the knowledge that, short-term, little is likely to emerge except, at best, the heightening of political awareness.) The former alternative almost always leads to a chain of ever-greater compromise whereby the committed socialist is worn down by the dead weight of a massive and bureaucratic party structure until, eventually, he or she becomes virtually indistinguishable from the average social democrat (cf. Bevan); whereas the latter alternative can lead at worst to the introverted sterility of sectarian warfare and a retreat into a totally unreal world of obscure personal and ideological dispute, and at best to an uphill process of Marxist educational and activist work removed from centres of power. (These are the short-term realities. Proponents of both strategies argue that long-term their positions are viable. This debate is followed up in the final Chapter.) On the national level, the stakes are, of course, that much higher but the dilemma remains basically the same: power (with compromise) or socialist politics (with no power).

Most, though by no means all, Marxists would argue that the Labour Party, at least in its present form, can never be a socialist party, in the Marxist sense.[77] The failure of all Labour left-wingers to push the Party into socialism testifies to the validity of this view. As has already been argued, the rout of the Left, which has been in progress since the inception of the LRC in 1900, is due to both ideological and structural factors. The crucial question for Marxists in terms of practical, political action is thus whether activity within the Labour Party can transform the Party or whether the task for socialists is to build an alternative.[78]

Marxists differ considerably in their analysis of the Labour Party's 'achievements' since its inception in 1900. Most accept that to a very large degree the civic freedoms enjoyed in the UK (which are too often either underrated or, worse, written off as 'bourgeois' freedoms) are the direct results of the struggles of the Labour Movement in nineteenth- and twentieth-century society. More controversial and divisive has been the analysis of the Labour Party's economic role; in particular, its progress on the conversion of the economic structure from a capitalist privately-owned system to a socialist publicly-owned system. As we have argued above (see pp. 57-8) the party's nationalization measures in the 1945-51 government have not resulted in a decisive move towards socialism: they have not even led to any significant redistribution of wealth or indeed of political or industrial power. In so far as the idea of public ownership has been put into practice—and the extent after 1948 has been demonstrably minimal—it has been on the Fabian, corporatist model discussed earlier. Few on the Left of the Party—and none of the Marxist critics outside the Party—are convinced of the Labour Party's commitment to public ownership in anything other than the Fabian sense; and increasingly this commitment reduces to a greater concentration upon co-operation between the State and private industry. Public ownership as the basis of the creation of a new socialist order—even of Fabian conception—has been to all intents and purposes abandoned.

In terms of attitudes the other major feature of 1945-51 (and indeed of the post-War period generally) has been the development of the so-called 'Welfare State'. Between 1945 and 1951 the institutionalization, through State agencies, of a wide variety of social welfare services was established.

This 'commitment to Welfare' was, as we have already noted, a policy objective shared by all sections of the Labour Movement. And in many senses few would deny that the Welfare State is 'a good thing'. Yet Marxists have made some serious qualifications: first of all it is worrying for Marxism that the provision of a Welfare State system can be accommodated within capitalism—there is nothing about the institution of a Welfare State which, of itself, threatens or interferes with capitalism. Thus, whilst not denying the benefits of socialized welfare, there is a danger within social democratic movements of supposing that the establishment of a Welfare State system (and its defence against Conservative and/or business attacks) is synonymous with the achievement of a socialist system. To make Welfare State provision the central part of a Socialist programme is to divert attention from the real power nexus of capitalism: the economic control of industrial and commercial organization by private ownership.

Indeed, there is an important sense in which the Welfare State can be seen as highly functional to the existence of capitalism: on the 'bread and circuses' argument the existence of a complex and wide-ranging system of benefits and welfare provision tends to cushion the greatest hardships produced by the economic system and thus lessen the potential for protest against that system. Thus, whereas in the 1930s unemployment meant near starvation, untold suffering *and* a fundamental questioning of the viability of capitalism by the 'intellectual strata' of society, in the economic crisis conditions of the 1970s the Welfare State unemployment benefit system and related legislation, has, at least to date, prevented any major expression of protest.

Perhaps most serious of all the Marxist reservations, there is abundant evidence[79] that the Welfare State is paid for by the working class. It is generally argued, particularly by the 'middle class' and by the Press, that the financing of the Welfare State system has meant a major shift in real disposable income from the 'rich' to the 'poor': that Welfare State financing (both through tax and National Insurance contributions) has in fact acted as a redistributive tax. This has been shown to be almost without foundation. Those who use the services by and large pay for them. The case for the extension of the Welfare State services *as a part of the Socialist project* is thus severely weakened.[80]

Marxists are agreed that the existing 'reformist' policies of the Labour Party can never produce a socialist system. Rather than acting as a political focal point for opposition to the capitalist system the Labour Party is increasingly acting, it is argued, as a crucial managing agent of that system: the essential and 'responsible' link between the private owners and managers of industry and commerce, and the economically powerful Trade Union movement. Only a party based on Marxist analysis and therefore determined to oppose the bourgeois parliamentary State (*and* the 'parliamentary cretinism' of Labourism) can begin to build a genuine socialist movement. Such a prognosis is justified, in Marxist terms, by the failure, over a relatively long period of time, of the British Labour Party to achieve a socialist perspective (let alone a socialist transformation). It can also point to more dramatic examples from the international history of the working class—one of the most recent and most important being the brutal, violent and (one fears) final overthrow of the Allende government in Chile. As Coates says at the end of his work on the Labour Party:[81]

> No ruling class in history has voluntarily surrendered its prerogatives and power. Rather such a class has (and invariably will) deploy the full range of its sanctions against any set of Parliamentarians bent on its destruction: sanctions rooted in its class position under capitalism, and stretching from administrative obstructionism through economic dislocation, financial movements, and ultimately to the use of force itself. If the extremities of these sanctions have not been seen in Britain, this is not because the ruling class here is more constitutionalist than sane. It is because the Labour Party has never seriously challenged its fundamental powers and prerogatives.

Such a position, arguing from a perspective of class analysis and based on the overriding need to create a mass revolutionary party, has little if any common ground with Left Labour views, let alone 'mainstream' social democracy of the Fabian type. All non-Marxists in the Labour movement are to some extent reformist[82]—following logically on the assumptions made about the fundamentally integrative nature of modern society, it is argued that the system is flexible, and capable of evolutionary reform: not only is reform possible, it is in the interest of the whole society. Moreover, social democrats argue, given the strength of British democratic traditions, reform should be relatively easy to achieve in institutional terms. Socialism has ceased to be on the agenda, although lip-service is occasionally paid, in vague rhetoric, to some of the 'socialist objectives' of the movement. There is a vast ideological gulf, too, between the old ILP Left (the 'Tribune' Left) and Marxists: the 'Tribune' Left are not merely trapped in the Parliamentary game—though this in itself is an immense handicap to political action. (This is especially true when a Labour government is in office: then the Left can always be called on to come to heel in order 'to keep the Tories out'.) The 'Tribune' group derives its ideology from the old moral crusading politics of the ILP, with a few additions of more 'hard-headed' pragmatism and Realpolitik gained over the decades of defeat and humiliation. But this means it has no overall perspective—in terms of analysis, objectives, or strategy. Amongst many other deficiencies, from a Marxist viewpoint, this has reduced the old socialist vision of Maxton, Lansbury (and even Hardie and

Political culture of contemporary Britain (2): social democracy

MacDonald) to a largely unrelated series of rearguard actions on welfare benefits, worker participation, unemployment, and whatever else crops up in the government's legislative programme.

Marxists thus criticize both groups within Labourism as being mistaken, fundamentally and irrevocably, about the nature of socialism and about the means of its attainment. Indeed, it may be argued, with Ralph Miliband, that the Labour Party acts as the supreme 'manager of discontent' in modern society: a safety valve which prevents rather than facilitates radical political development.

The role of the Labour Movement, for Marxists, should therefore be to mobilize the working class politically (and industrially) to change this system by force; the role which the Labour Movement is in fact fulfilling is to legitimate the existing capitalist system to the working class. Social democracy has so thoroughly permeated the Labour Movement—and has become so integral and acceptable a part of modern capitalist society—that the Labour Party has become, for most Marxists, a positively counter-productive force in the context of the struggle for socialism.

The acceptability of social democracy to the 'general public'—psychologically as much as politically—has been gained at the expense of throwing out socialism altogether. The crucial question for Marxists thus becomes, as we argued at the beginning of this section, how does capitalist society 'legitimate' its values and therefore its structure? And, within this context, how has the Labour Movement become an integral and supportive part of capitalist structure rather than a critical and alternative basis for the creation of a socialist alternative? This question of legitimacy—and of what determines the 'level of consciousness'—has become crucial for Marxists. But this area is also of key importance across a whole range of disciplines and interests, not least in social work. What is it that determines the norms within which social work operates and how should the social worker respond to these norms? And, bearing in mind the discussion in this chapter, what are the links between these norms and the political culture of our society?

These problems centre on the concept of 'legitimation' and the various analyses put forward from differing ideological positions to explain the way in which our social structure is, by and large, acceptable to the population. Before turning to this, however, we must relate these political considerations more directly to social work objectives and methods.

Chapter five

Political directions in social work

A social worker specializing in welfare rights described his role as combining traditional social casework with efforts to influence local and ultimately central government policy, where that policy impinged on his client's situation. Such a breadth of social work functions is at first sight almost arrogant in its implicit claims, but on reflection indicates the interdependent areas that involve social workers, employers and their clients. The profession's origins lie in *ad hoc* efforts to resolve crises of the day and from some of these efforts stem one of the elements of the genericism of social work. It is somewhat ironic that orthodox social caseworkers were criticized, sometimes unfairly, for implying, or allowing it to be implied, that the casework method was a cure-all for both personal and social problems, while in practice concentrating only upon the personal. (This extreme view is almost a tenet of faith for some critics of casework,[1] despite many qualifying statements to the contrary—for example, Richmond[2] in the 1920s and Nursten, Perlman[3] and Hollis[4] more recently.) Yet now the new social worker appears to embrace even wider claims, incorporating not only casework, but also group and community work and social action. Perhaps one of the reasons for this almost accidental drift towards a professional omnipotence lies in the rag-bag of tasks given to social workers. With such a range of functions where should social workers look for a disciplined theoretical framework to provide a viable reference point? The complexity of this problem and the lack of any immediately identifiable 'knowledge base' has resulted all too often in social workers adopting an *ad hoc*, pragmatic approach and dismissing 'theory' as irrelevant. We have already argued that there are general ideological connotations inherent in such a 'pragmatic' approach; in the social work context it is also important to emphasize both the theoretical insights and the hard information available from a number of academic fields which may act as guides to action for the social worker.[5]

Political directions in social work

As a starting point, we must consider the various 'knowledge bases' which can claim to provide social work with some theoretical framework so as to be better able to understand social work's wider involvement and its links with the political culture of society.

Knowledge is, of course, relative and can never be absolute, though this truism is probably more modern than is realized. No longer do we believe that through increased scientific expertise the objective factual 'truth' within the natural and social sciences can be discovered.[6] For it is now accepted that there is no bedrock of objective fact in any of the social sciences. In social work the epistemological situation is even more tentative and diffuse: there is no undisputed theoretical framework, no immutable reference points. Nevertheless, social work derives most of its theory from four major areas of study: sociology, psychology, social administration and politics.[7] It is in these disciplines that is to be found the amalgam of social work's task; to understand, and despite social work ambivalence, influence, the individual's relationship with himself, his family and wider society—and simultaneously, to comprehend the reciprocal interaction of the social worker, agency and society upon those people categorized as clients. Not surprisingly social work is in an uneasy situation as it attempts to translate both individual theoretical propositions and more difficult, overall theoretical perspectives into personalized professional action. The abstractions and generalizations of the social sciences were not intended as field manuals for practising social workers. The imprecision of the research in the social and behavioural sciences is well known (e.g. it has been observed[8] that all methodologies so far used in assessing the commonality of the child-parent interaction contain serious limitations and biases, which both researcher and 'therapist' must make explicit and attempt to limit). The problems of applying to the individual situation sociological information gained through group surveys are notorious. The inadequacies of the professional's perception have already been noted[9] and social work still awaits accurate techniques that are equivalent to the medical measurements of pulse, respiration and blood pressure. The imbalance between the daily life-and-death decisions which the social worker makes and the paucity and unreliability of the information available in the context of a specific situation, both explains, and partially constitutes, the nature of the relationship between the social sciences and social work. At most, social work can use the information garnered from the formal disciplines of the social sciences, psychology and sociology; this information is then put into practice in a context where formal disciplines are often not only irrelevant but counter-productive and even dangerous. Perhaps the best example of such a situation is that found with the 'baby battering' syndrome; careful consideration of all the evidence suggests a highly complex multifactorial causation,[10] while one of the largest clinical studies done in the UK[11] would lead the unsuspecting social worker to believe that only the lower socio-economic groups are likely to abuse their children: a patently untrue and absurd belief as any experienced 'child-care' or 'child psychiatric' social worker would know.

Without entering into the heated controversy over the degree of objectivity in the social sciences all would surely agree that in the case of social work, a value system (more often than not couched in terms of social and political ideology) forms the general framework of decision-making within which the social worker defines both his overall role and his specific course of action. Whether this paradigm is consciously or unconsciously utilized is, as we have already stressed, immaterial in this context. In Chapters 3 and 4 we discussed ways in which the development of British political culture has resulted in the current divergence of socio-political perspectives in contemporary Britain; we must now relate this to social work practice.

The political context of social work—its intimate involvement with decisions at all levels about social priorities, its central and crucial position in the wide-ranging argument about the potential for radical change through reformism and its importance in the perpetual dilemma between concern for the individual and structural societal change—makes the political base of social work of prime importance.

Knowledge of social policy and administration must also form an important part of the social worker's intellectual equipment. For good or ill our society functions increasingly through large and complex administrative structures and the framework within which the social worker operates is vital in determining not only structure but policy itself. (This is not to say that problems of bureaucracy, centralism and administrative control are peculiar to the UK—or indeed to advanced capitalist countries. One has only to reflect on the problems of bureaucracy in the USSR, the history of the cultural revolution in China and the problems of corrupt administrations in Latin America, to acknowledge that these are truly international developments and are not peculiar to any single society or ideology.)

Just as medicine has been criticized for its lack of social and political awareness,[12] so social work, unless it can consciously and methodologically analyse its theoretical framework and then determine its future direction, will fall into the trap of fulfilling a mechanistic and purely organizational role in society, responding to the dominant value-system rather than interacting with and changing the pattern of the social structure. Social work may well involve the use of academic disciplines and analytical skills but it must above all else develop a prescriptive role. It is to a discussion of what the precise nature of that prescriptive role should be that the remainder of this book is devoted.

The duality and multi-directional aspect of social work

An examination of the political directions of social work leads us to emphasize again the basic duality inherent in all social work practice: individual care versus societal change or control, a variation on a theme common to all major political theories. When discussing the development of the British political culture earlier, we saw how the place of the individual in industrial society had been a central question for the past 200 years. Within all the major Western political traditions—Conservative, Liberal, Social Democratic and Marxist—constant attention has been given to the supposed or actual loss of individual freedom in our society. The dual developments of corporate state tendencies and of an increasing emphasis upon regionalism, community action, workers' control, etc., bear witness to the central problem posed by this precarious and strained balance in our existing form of society. What does this mean for social work?

If and when individual social break-down occurs, social work is one of the increasingly important means of repair and its mediation is called for by a society which seeks to protect and/or *control* its vulnerable and/or deviant members.[13] Alternatively, people themselves *initiate* support to redress a balance that threatens their personal and social identity. In this situation the problem for social work is how and on which 'side' to intervene. Should the emphasis be upon the person or society? And this must again take us back to the wider and more complex issues of the conflicting analyses through which the true interests of the individual and society are interpreted.[14]

In an earlier chapter the various theoretical models generally used by social workers were touched upon. It was noted that dependent upon the criteria used, methods of intervention evolved. These paradigms were not mutually exclusive but there was a tendency for one of the themes to predominate in either agency function, and the legislation underlying it, or in the orientation of the social worker. It is self-evident that social workers will be influenced by their professional background, though this is complicated by the existence of a large proportion of social workers who are untrained. This is exemplified by studies in the area of child fostering[15] and by complaints about the lack of specificity in the training of those working with the mentally ill,[16] and of problems of the education welfare officer.[17] In practice, there is a tendency for the 'conservative' element in the social work and local authority hierarchy to be reinforced by the untrained who are likely to be more uncritical of the senior 'trained' worker. Nevertheless, there are probably much deeper divisions within the whole of social work which stem from fundamentally distinct *ideological* positions—even if these ideological perspectives are not overt and explicit. It may be, therefore, that in some areas of work the dominant theme would be determined not by what might be considered appropriate to that particular circumstance but rather by the exigencies of the service.

Whatever the specific factors involved two important general principles emerge: first, the frames of reference within which social workers operate differ significantly and affect not only attitudes but concrete action; and second, these frames of reference are intimately related to the overall ideological climate of society. By examining the content of the four frames of reference—the moral-ethical, the psycho-pathological, the psycho-social and the radical-political— and the ways in which these specifically social work frameworks are related to the wider social and political structure, it will be possible to present more clearly the options that are open to client, society and social worker.

The moral-ethical view point is based essentially upon a humanitarian and compassionate view of 'man in trouble'. Arguably such a sympathetic response would be natural and appropriate in any form of society. Implicit in this approach is the assumption that by chance or perhaps because of inherent genetic factors, the origin of the problem is primarily individually based; misfortune has come to a fellow human being who must be comforted and given asylum. More cynically, one might add that from society's point of view, the emphasis is in practice upon misfits being 'tidied away' so as to avoid the community being exposed to distressing and conscience-provoking situations. In one sense this is a very modern approach to sickness or poverty, for it assumes a functional sociological position, implying that the normal person would not choose to be 'ill' or 'sick' or in any other way 'deviant'. In the nineteenth century, it would generally have been assumed that a person in distress was in some way negligent or even sinful, and only those who showed a proper sense of repentance were deserving of help. Hence the development of the concept of the 'deserving poor' which still has some influence in modern British social legislation.[18] Both the nineteenth and twentieth centuries' perspectives have a common assumption: that the task of the social worker is to alleviate individual suffering. To some extent the differences in the two causal explanations result from differing conceptions of Christianity: the one broadly emphasizing justice and rewards to those who strive for the 'good life', and the other, the compassion and the 'love thy neighbour' aspect of the Christian moral code. What is important, in the social work context, is that many social workers with a Christian orientation *perceive* the social and moral implications of Christianity as leading to one or the other of the above formulations and take action accordingly.[19] The key corollary of this assumption lies in the belief that the cause of the problem lies *within* the individual, not external to him and intervention methods are posited accordingly. Consequently, little if any importance is attached to social and environmental factors and it is argued that the solution of the specific problem can be effected by individually focused treatment. This approach is thought by its advocates to be both essentially apolitical and 'practical'. 'While others are theorizing we are actually helping people' is a frequent comment, and while laudable in its way this approach is, again, open to all the dangers of 'abstracted empiricism'. Moreover, with its avowed concentration on the individual, to the virtual exclusion of societal and ideological factors, the approach is in reality deeply conservative. For while the 'body' is often recognized as important (Salvationists, for example, have a long tradition of 'social caring'), it is nevertheless the 'soul' that is the prime target. The social environment—the political institutions, the economic system, the dominant norm system and so on—are taken as given and implicitly immutable. Consequently 'worth-while' and 'realistic' changes, in the social work context, can only come about through individually based solutions. Life can thus be neatly compartmentalized—and the problems of the client be separated from the wider, and more complex, social and ideological issues.

This attitude to social work is of course highly political, a fact supported by such unlikely authorities as the Bishop of Liverpool, David Sheppard,[20] while Western readers need to remember just how atypical are such writers as Illich and Freire.[21] By generally ignoring social factors the moral-ethical viewpoint in effect accepts the *status quo*, institutionally and culturally, and normally denies the relevance of social reform. The subjective motivation is often Christian in inspiration and genuinely humanitarian in practice; but the objective criteria for action *and* the effects of such social work motivations must be inherently conservative and will normally tend to reinforce the *status quo*.[22]

The end result of this perspective is the acceptance of the paternalistic Conservative State as the macrocosmic context in which the microcosmic 'good works' take place, whilst leaving the structure, policies and long-term aims of social work to be determined by this State. Despite the sincerity and value of the philanthropic tradition, from Lord Shaftesbury to the present day, the moral-ethical approach must, in the contemporary context, result in a social work that is at best reactionary and of minimal social impact.

The psycho-pathological approach is at first sight another apparently apolitical typology of social work. The paradigm evolved from the psycho-analytically oriented school of social work which had developed from clinical work involving predominantly middle-class patients. This latter aspect has tended to alienate the more 'radical' social worker, who considers any approach basing itself upon middle-class situations and values to be at best only marginally relevant. The progression of unhappy people to the doors of Freudian clinics is well known; what requires to be appreciated by late twentieth-century therapists is that the Freudian school was at its inception a truly liberating, humane and rational approach to the tragedies of the human condition. An over-simplistic dismissal of the work of these pioneers does little justice to them and indicates a serious misunderstanding of their position and a *post facto* prejudice. Because the dynamic school was so individualistic and the predominant social and political culture was at least superficially amenable to this appeal, doctors and social workers of the 1940s and 1950s found this a progressive framework, acceptable to 'public opinion'. But as so often happens, the new remedy became the panacea for all ills and was massively over-extended. Within a decade expectations were beginning to be replaced by disappointment and rejection, and the baby was lost with the proverbial bathwater. The psycho-pathological model assumes that the problematic behaviour stems from intra-psychic conflict which attenuates personality development and normal functioning. (It may be that in this context the most serious criticism of Freudian ideas was the assumption of an ideal norm; failure to achieve this was considered due to immaturity or pathological tendencies. The result of these basic assumptions has led many Freudians to have a pessimistic and essentially static concept of human nature.) If, however, the unhappiness and maladaptive behaviour does come from unresolved psychic conflicts, then the logical response is to discover the underlying causes, bring them to consciousness and expose them to rational analysis. This cathartic experience then cleans 'the stuffed bosom of that perilous stuff that weighs heavy upon the heart' (*Macbeth*). However, the limitations of such an approach become evident in dealing with 'Mrs Smith', wife of an unemployed labourer with six children, living in a 2 up and 2 down when, in a parody of rational analysis, the problem might be seen in Oedipal terms, as Mrs Smith emasculated her husband by becoming pregnant and therefore making him appear less adequate! Such interpretations probably never happened, and are manifestly absurd, but they do demonstrate the point that this approach can so easily ignore all the evidence of accumulative socio-economic deprivation that Wedge and Prosser, amongst others, so aptly describe.[23] Obviously there are direct political and economic problems that require resolution to enable 'Mrs Smith' to escape what Sir Keith Joseph has described as the 'cycle of deprivation'; (though there are serious criticisms of this concept which, it is argued, in effect still leaves the 'stigma' of the inadequacies upon the individual rather than recognizing the inherent contribution of the socio-economic system).[24] It is, of course, self-evident that these adverse social circumstances carry many psychological concomitants which lead to the defensive apathy and depression of many clients.[25] It does seem that the inherent weakness of the psycho-pathological style of social work lies in its primary emphasis upon the individual which is somewhat out of touch with the growing collectivist social environment of the late twentieth century. On the ideological level there has been a marked shift away from the crude individualism of the early nineteenth century in all schools of social and political thought. This move away from individualism—economically, culturally and politically—towards collectivism, is challenged by none of the major ideological frameworks, although the interpretations of this change and its causation are, of course, a matter of dispute. (Incidentally the 'new' Conservative rhetorical support for individualism has yet to be translated into political action.) It is anachronistic to reconstruct the exclusive individualism of the psycho-pathological approach in a society where external social and political constraints are generally agreed to have become so dominant. The oversimplification and hence distortion of Freudian ideas which this approach has brought to social work has exacerbated this individualistic exclusivity and discredited the whole perspective. It is however important, though perhaps unfashionable, to stress that in our opinion the type of help available via this approach will always be required—in any conceivable form of society. Consider the situation of the mother with the dead child and the guilt that so often accompanies such a tragedy, or the parents who are over-protective (for quite non-social reasons), or the family with the severely physically or mentally handicapped child—all these require in-depth counselling to help with the complex emotions and interpersonal problems that so often follow such situations.

Having added this important caveat however, the basic argument remains: both the moral-ethical and psycho-pathological perspectives deny, by omission, any concern with the need to consider societal restructuring for the benefit of those people whom they are in business to aid; as we have argued, this perspective is inherently, albeit often unconsciously, conservative and ultimately ineffectual, as it ignores the wider areas within which social work operates.

These perspectives are thus, in our view, limited and based upon fundamentally unacceptable assumptions.

The psycho-social or socio-psychological approach indicates in its title its theoretical origins: it is an attempt to bring together the emotional and social factors that operate within people's lives. It was given a strong impetus first by Karen Horney[26] who wished to broaden out from the Freudian concern with the purely psychological; and this in turn led to what is broadly described as the ego-dynamic school, which, while still concerned with the individual, sees the interaction of social and emotional factors as being equally relevant.[27] The work of Rogers[28] has strongly influenced these developments, and the resulting social work and psycho-therapy are attractive to a wide range of social workers, in large part because of the focus upon the individual *and* the family. The psycho-socially oriented worker can thus focus upon the psychological effects of social pressure, or vice versa, or on the interaction between the two. The strength of this position is being reasserted in a more conscious social way by such teachers as Rapoport and Perlman[29] in the USA, and a number of seemingly unlikely adherents in the UK.[30] Perlman[31] offers a particularly useful psycho-social continuum when she categorizes three areas of difficulty: clients suffering because of socio-economic deficits, those whose relationships are distorted, and those whose lives are disrupted and disturbed (this latter group might be broadly associated with what is understood as psychosis). Thus this type of social worker legitimately finds himself working with clients whose problems are external in origin, as well as dealing with people whose difficulties are primarily problems of interpersonal relationships. This framework, it is suggested, is the predominant one for most social caseworkers; such a direction re-emphasises the 'social' in social work without losing sight of the needs of the individual.

Criticism of this approach has centred upon the contention that the techniques have become 'pseudo-scientific'[32] and over-mystified into a professionalism that is a form of social control. This may well be a danger, potential or actual; but the advantages of the approach are considerable: it is essentially a personal perspective which allows varying degrees of human interaction in which sympathy, concern, compassion and a desire for justice and social change can be expressed. Recently, the psycho-social casework approach has received some unexpected support from radicals, who while implacably opposed to the existing capitalist social system, remind social workers that they must not develop social work into yet another form of bureaucratic exploitation. It is said that social casework is an effort to stem the 'de-humanizing' spirit within the Welfare State that presses for organizational efficiency, often at the expense of the individual.³³ Both Cohen and Pearson wish to focus upon the radical - political model of social work but find that such an approach may tend to ignore and undervalue the individual experience of poverty, suffering, etc. If the need to work for and with individuals is referred to the periphery and replaced only by a concern with macro-cosmic social and political change, then there is a grave danger of further individual suffering resulting from the 'grand plan' to achieve socialism. Nowhere is the dilemma more acute for the social worker than in this context, where individual welfare may well conflict with social needs and ideological conviction.

The radical-political perspective of social work essentially sees the majority of the problems of poverty and its attendant evils as a structural necessity within capitalist society. Like the earlier orientations outlined this is not a self-contained, cohesive theoretical 'school', but a loose alliance of radically motivated groups who are left of centre and perhaps united only in their dislike of the present state of society and social work. Yet social work, certainly in this century, has always had elements of the radical and political, albeit usually of the reformist type. Indeed, British, unlike American, social work, had its origins in piecemeal, but *radical* legislation, which, while reformist in aim, sought to achieve major changes in society.³⁴ The social work theories developed in the USA were all based on the assumption that the existing social and political system was both stable (if not static) and generally desirable (if not perfect)—a fundamental difference between the ethos of the same profession in the two countries! However, whether the creation of the Welfare State and its extension, is part of the socialist restructuring process, is a complex argument, and is discussed in more detail in Chapters 4 and 6.

There would be general agreement that many people defined as social work clients are in reality the victims of a socio-economic system[35] that requires either major reform or complete re-structuring. This group of social workers ranges from people such as Briar and Miller,[36] two of the seminal critics of casework and social work, who argue for advocacy and reformist social work roles—to Leonard and Mayo[37] who argue that such reformist positions can quickly become absorbed as part of the very system that they originally set out to challenge.

Marxists have, of course, much to say about how social work is practised and what its aims should be. Lees described the militant or revolutionary social worker as someone who becomes concerned with 'participatory politics' as a 'means of increasing awareness rather than achieving any particular piecemeal reform. The real goal is social revolution.'[38] This approach derives from a wider analysis of social and political structure which, amongst other things, sees no hope of 'reformist measures' effectively influencing the present system (see Chapter 4). Marxist social workers thus see 'piecemeal reform' as at best of marginal importance in their long-term strategy. This is not to say that Marxists should be unconcerned with the humanitarian aspects of social work, but rather that these should be seen as providing short-term individual amelioration and should not be elevated to the status of long-term strategy. Marxists see a major and highly important function of social workers as being the raising of the level of consciousness of the communities in which they work—initially by making people more aware of the exploitative nature of existing society.

Following on from this argument, social work is further criticized for its function as a bridgehead between the established institutionalized forces of the State and an alienated and potentially hostile section of the community. From this viewpoint the political function of traditional social work has been, and is, to legitimate society's existing system to its most deprived and exploited people. In this sense, it is argued by Marxists, social work fulfils a function not unlike that of the Labour Party which 'takes the major role in the management of discontent and helps to keep it within safe bounds'.[39] This argument is of considerable importance and is discussed further in Chapters 6 and 7.

With social work being essentially a practical activity, and British social and political culture having strong empirical and pragmatic tendencies, it is hardly surprising that these radical-political arguments are often rejected as irrelevant theorizing. As Cohen succinctly puts it, social workers often feel like 'telling the sociologists and political theorists . . . it's all right for you to talk, we have to work where the heat is.'[40]

The crucial question of analysis cannot, however, be brushed off so lightly, whatever political-social opinion one holds. It is one of the main arguments, albeit an obvious one, of this book that blind pragmatism in social work, as in all other activities, is fatal: the social worker cannot orient himself to his work until he has clarified his objectives and this he cannot do until he has analysed the problems he is dealing with and the context in which these problems occur. The moral-ethical social worker is just as ideological as the Marxist social worker: if anything, more so, because he is not *conscious* of the ideological framework within which he is operating. The ideological differences over general orientation and priorities is an important question that will be returned to in succeeding chapters.

As already mentioned, the social worker operates at the point of tension between the individual and society. By definition the social worker is concerned with social functioning and the sanctions, both implicit and explicit, in society. Pearson,[41] in a rather extreme exploration of this problem, described the social worker as an industrial deviant, who, if he were a 'good' social worker, would act on behalf of his client against either agency policy or even, if necessary, 'society'. The CCETSW stated in an authoritative, if somewhat vague, way that social workers can operate only within areas sanctioned by society;[42] yet even if for most orthodox practitioners Pearson's view, that social workers might well be justifiably involved in showing people how to break the law, is untenable, the position is always debatable. The issue is not whether all laws should always be obeyed, but rather the ambivalent position in which social work is placed—on the one hand, a representative of the established order, and on the other, a radically anti-authority force in society.[43] With a few notable exceptions (e.g. in Latin America) other analogous professions, doctors, priests, and lawyers, side with the forces of the existing system.[44]

What direction is social work likely to take, and how can the duality of the micro-macro tension be resolved? In the light of the earlier discussions on the different orientations of social work, we must now turn to a discussion of the aims of social work, in essence, what is social work in business for—to comfort, to change, to control or to promote social conflict?

Bearing in mind the earlier arguments which described the development of British political culture we can now consider the socio-political aspects of social work practice and attempt to tease out the inherent and conflicting themes. The apparent contradictions create confusion at all social work levels and defy the establishment of a coherent theoretical framework. The various types of social work might be seen, not as an orthodoxy, nor even as segmental[45] (though this latter is a very useful concept), but rather as having four distinct directional thrusts seeking to achieve equally distinctive but at times, over-lapping, goals. The four directional elements are, however, based upon a set of values and theories as to the nature of man and society, some compatible, and some not. The recognition of these separate elements thus allows an understanding of variations in social work and partially accounts for the misunderstandings that arise amongst social workers, and between social workers and their agencies. Figure 5.1 (p. 81) illustrates the point being made—that social work's aims are concerned with comfort, change, control and conflict, and at times a mixture of all four.

Change

It would seem that irrespective of method or orientation all social workers agree that social work is about change. Authorities as diverse as Hollis, Towle, Perlman, Leonard and Pearson, all direct their methods towards bringing about change in people's lives. On a broader front, the 'welfare service delivery' DHSS approach, personified by Sir Keith Joseph, wishes to create a milieu which would allow clients of the SSD a new opportunity to lead a fuller life. Given Sir Keith's position on the Right of the Conservative party, it can be seen that 'change' in social work is accepted right across the political spectrum, although the sort and extent of change desired varies considerably. The issue is not *whether* to change but in what direction and at what pace. Thus, dependent upon the frame of reference adopted, the social worker following the analysis of the situation must also decide which of the other functions of social work—comfort, control or conflict, is to be given priority.

If the social worker's focus is primarily psychological, then his intervention may discourage any moves into the social, political or economic fields. Conversely, a predominantly 'socially' focused worker may well be restricted by *the client* who feels that his 'problem' is emotionally based and may reject the perception of the social worker as irrelevant—a point made by a number of writers.[46] It is not unusual to find that the social worker desires to obtain social and financial rights for the client, but is blocked by the client who is embarrassed or ashamed of 'making a fuss'. Hence, communication between client and worker is of paramount importance if any mutual understanding is to be achieved.

The criteria used by the social worker to decide upon objectives for change are crucial. The political issue can be clearly seen if the social worker asks Titmuss's basic question[47] regarding the result of any welfare policy: who is the primary beneficiary?—the individual, his family, the neighbourhood, or society? If the answer is all four then the social worker need have no fear that he is exploiting or deceiving anyone, least of all his client; however, if one of the groups is excluded from the advantages of the service then the social worker needs to decide for whom he is acting. It is even more complex to determine what is in the best interests of the four groups, both in the short- *and* long-term. The answer must ultimately depend upon which frame of reference is finally adopted.

It was stated earlier that society assumes that a 'professional' assessment will be neutral and unbiased and the trust in the professional is based on the belief that the individual need fear no exploitation and the 'client's good' will be the only criterion that influences the social worker. Yet professionalism may well be the thin veil masking deep differences of perception and value, as has been exemplified in studies on teachers, doctors and social workers. To claim 'professional objectivity' is not only spurious but dangerous.⁴⁸ This problem has even affected the newer methods of social work; for example, community workers are appreciating that they can also exploit their clients, if only by sacrificing clients to ideological positions.⁴⁹ The situation in which a local authority finds its own employees (e.g. community workers) actively engaged in stimulating community opposition to the authority's policies, is becoming quite common-place.

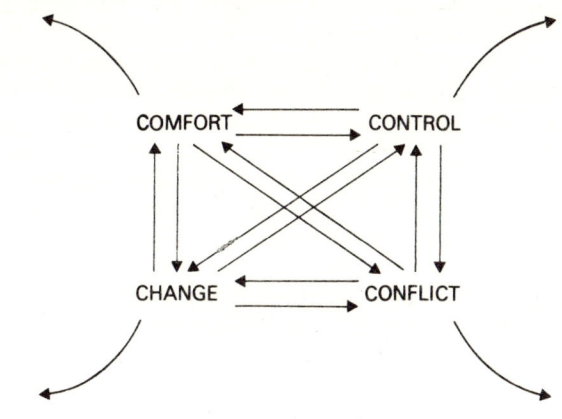

```
           COMFORT ←——→ CONTROL

           CHANGE  ←——→ CONFLICT
```

Figure 5.1

This situation highlights one of the central dilemmas for radical social workers, and indeed for radically inclined employees in any State-controlled institution. Beyond a fairly limited level it is unrealistic to expect public bodies, which are by definition committed to the preservation of the present system, to accept what they regard as consistent and deliberate subversion. The feasibility of changing the orientations of such institutions is a central debate on the Left— whether the context is social work, universities, industry (or even the Labour Party!).

Whatever position is taken, the fact remains that in social work generally and community work in particular, there is likely to be inherent and continuous conflict, at least in the short term, between underprivileged groups in the community and the 'apparatus of the State'. The social worker must decide where he stands, partly on *ad hoc* grounds but ultimately upon criteria derived from a wider social and political analysis.

In the practical work situation the social worker does in fact operate with a large degree of unofficial discretion. Working on a declared, or more often implicit, value system, the social worker has to, and is expected to, take sides. For example, if a client is homosexual and his lover is just under the legal age of consent, it is probable that the majority of social workers would ignore such a border-line situation, assuming of course that the younger person was not being exploited in any way. In taking no action the social worker may be making a judgment upon the law as it relates to an individual. The paradox is that in all probability 'society' would wish the social worker to exercise such discretion, provided that it was not known elsewhere, thus avoiding examining the issue of individual behaviour versus societal norms.

'Change' appears to be acceptable to all social workers, but what sort of change? It is here that the 'normal' apolitical, or social democratic, social worker should become aware of the trap of his comfortable, individually based, value system. He believes that a society such as ours, generally considered to be broadly democratic, has undergone fundamental reform and is capable of such further reform as is necessary. He has to be case-specific by virtue of his training and society's expectation, yet the 'task-to-be-accomplished' holds mutually incompatible features. Just as it was necessary to ask about the focus of intervention in relation to the changing situation, the question must also be asked, who and what *defines* the task. This leads to the prior problem of deciding whether the way in which the task is defined and implemented is rational. The rationality is likely to be directly related to the psycho-socio-political aspects involved in a particular case and in behaviour which appears to have certain common aetiological or presenting factors. Often the label given indicates nothing more than a piece of behaviour; the 'diagnosis' gives no prescription for action because the individual case produced that behaviour for a variety of reasons, as, for example, in 'baby battering'. (However, in these emergency situations it is accepted that the first priority must be to safeguard the child against further damage, and by doing so, protect the parent from the possible consequences of the impulse ridden actions). But while such cases may have clear operational directions, the 'syndrome' is so complex that social workers may well act in quite different ways, despite the fact that different participants collectively created the same tragic end-product: a hurt child.[50] This confuses the 'layman' who may complain that social workers are being either too interfering, or too easy going. It is here that the problem of 'professional freedom' reappears, for if the ascribed task is seen to be and can be shown to be, less than reason-based, then the professional has the responsibility to explain to society, in practice the SSD committee and the courts, *why* a certain course of action was taken.[51]

The radical-political social worker may argue that the subsidiary task is to gain the active co-operation of a reluctant client and persuade him of the need for publicity to highlight the plight of others as well as himself. It is clear that both the radical and the traditional social worker can abuse their trust and act for their own interests. For some social workers the true interests of the individual cannot be divorced from the wider social analysis: they will see the true interest as coterminous with social action, even if this entails short-term problems for the individual—for others such an argument would be highly suspect, because of its possible subjugation of 'individual' to 'ideological' objectives.[52]

Comfort

From the field of medicine comes the phrase, 'to harm never, to cure sometimes, to comfort always'. This would be acceptable to many social workers. In terms of social welfare delivery, such a response suggests immediate acceptance of the need to bring comfort.

For the social caseworker comfort is also probably a self-evident type of service. It is today accepted, and rightly so, that the caseworker should be directly involved with the client's material well-being, but he also offers a service beyond this, of a personal involvement.[53] In a few situations, however, the social caseworker may feel that emotional comfort may not be an immediate goal as there is some evidence to suggest that this discomfort is a spur to resolve the underlying problem.[54] Nevertheless the social caseworker would hope ultimately to ameliorate the client's situation and bring comfort. On the other hand the community worker may find 'comfort' something of a hindrance if he is seeking to encourage either major change or evaluation. Man is motivated by many things, sometimes the drive to hold on to a comfortable position, but the experienced worker knows that when he is in a deprived area, complacency, fear, intimidation and defensive apathy are some of his greatest enemies: the attitude of 'better the devil you know' brings its own brand of comfort! Hence the community worker approaches a 'comfortable' situation with the greatest caution.

Control

Control is a controversial concept in social work circles. Yet, eschewing the concept of control which leads to an uncritical obedience, the idea of appropriate limits has its protagonists.[55] For the welfare worker control is construed as avoiding a deterioration in the client's situation, often to prevent the need for residential care, whether for children or old people. The person who is *non compos mentis* because of a delusional state may require compulsory controlling care in his own interests or for the direct safety of others. No civilized society can fail to have some caring and humane method of controlling and protecting such people until such time as they are able to undertake their own care. The possible abuse or over-use of such 'powers' does not release any caring society from its obligations to contain and protect both the individual concerns and society at large.[56]

Proposals for ending compulsory powers for the care of people who cannot care for themselves are nonsensical and often stem from an insensitive ignorance and arrogance. For example, the elderly widower with a sudden chest condition may rapidly become confused and behave in a psychotic way; he may refuse help, and he will very likely die, unless a tranquillizer is administered and the necessary antibiotics given. His 'right' to live or die is not at issue because he is literally not in a fit state to decide. Of course, all social workers are involved in some 'control' situations, however the boundaries are blurred, for outside the obviously physically disabling conditions, the definitions of what should be controlled and who should control become less clear. Controversy rages as fiercely as ever over the treatment of those described as 'mentally ill' and, though this lies outside the scope of this text, there is a need to establish the idea of a 'rational' control that is genuinely rational, humane and individually based.

The probation service has, of course, a long tradition of straddling the divide between being a controlling agent and also being the advocate and protector; the social worker in the SSD is just beginning to be aware of the vast powers conferred, especially by recent legislation, which affect citizens at every stage of life. (For example, babies, infants and children under the Children Acts 1948 and 1975, and the Children and Young Persons Act 1963 and 1969, plus the Education Act 1944; parts of the National Assistance Act within the Social Security Act 1966, part of the National Health Service Act 1946 and the Mental Health Act 1959, for adults of all ages.) The social worker is authorized, under the various Acts, to enter homes, separate children from their families and institute a range of compulsory institutional admissions, and he may also legally advise and direct overt law enforcement agencies. These wide-ranging powers make the usual scapegoat of psychiatry look relatively ineffectual!

It may be argued that control *per se* is not necessarily bad providing that it is genuinely appropriate to the person's interests. The difficulty is that often social workers have to act not on 'evidence' of actual behaviour but on an assessment based upon *potential* behaviour. The social worker may be caught in the dilemma of an open-ended situation where concern for the particular client conflicts with the pressure from an often reactionary and usually ill-informed public opinion, responding to adverse publicity over a specific situation (e.g. G. Young).[57]

Again the issue turns in practice upon the frame of reference used by social work when it operates in the area of control. Dependent upon this analysis will be the *ways* in which social workers decide to exercise control and the *ends* they hope to achieve. Should social deviants, for example, be controlled in order to preserve the existing norm dominance? Or should social work act as a progressive force to change these norms? Such questions are not susceptible to answer without reference to the initial analysis.

Control is, of course, regarded with suspicion by all those who hold to the central societal (and social work) value system of social democracy, raising as it does the spectre of the totalitarian Orwellian thought police. And yet our system demands an ever-greater degree of cultural homogeneity to avoid the dangers of social conflict. To what extent this control is exercised by institutional agencies under the aegis of the State, such as the education system, and potentially social work, is another crucial area of discussion. This and other aspects of legitimation are explored in Chapter 6.

Conflict

What are the possibilities of social work being involved with the final area of possible social work aims: conflict? The idea of the social worker as an advocate between authority and client was developed in the late 1960s and several writers[58] have urged the value of this method, especially in the training of new social workers. This must result in a potential conflict situation where social workers actively avoid, ignore or break the law—or more often encourage others to do so. Equally, simply by representing their clients in an Inquiry or Appeal, at which another department of their own local authority is represented against their clients, brings the social worker into direct confrontation with his employing authority and by implication, with the State.

The conflict perspective is, of course, most relevant to those who hold a Marxist or quasi-Marxist position. For the Marxist the *ultimate function* of social work must be to raise community, and thus ultimately political, consciousness by exposing the assumed class nature of existing society at both the local and national level. The greater the 'awareness' the greater the potential for conflict between working-class activists and 'authority'. This conflict orientation is thus couched in highly political terms and its acceptance must be conditional on a thorough-going Marxist analysis of social structure. For social democrats conflict has a much more restricted use and is above all basically concerned with protecting the rights of the individual against authority, not as a part of an overall political strategy, but as a basic principle of social and political justice.

Let us recapitulate the argument and present it in a tabular flow chart (see Table 5.1). The types of social work that have emerged are a reflection of the values and theories held of man and society; this leads to particular methods of social work which in time are linked to broad social work aims. These then illustrate something of the assumed nature of the society in which social work actually operates. It is not suggested that the chart outlines are mutually exclusive but rather that they act as broad indicators of the likely directional thrusts of social work and the attendant attitudes and political positions held. It is this very fluidity between methods, societal assumptions and resulting political orientation that is the background for the divisions within social work in the UK today. The problem for every level of social worker, whether Director or basic grade social worker, is that the diverse objectives are often unrecognized not only because of lack of clarity of professional assessments, or even prescribed tasks, but because aspects of all the perspectives may be shared by all. Consequently, the particular social worker may assume that because there is harmony in one area of social work, with his Director, agency or colleagues, then all that individual social worker's assumptions are shared.

Cynics have stressed the danger that social work may become a part of a 'mind police' that is much more effective than naked oppression, while on the other hand, politicians of the Right speak of dangerous subversive elements exploiting the young and vulnerable.[59]

These diverse perspectives exemplify both the ambivalent position of social work and the wide divergence of views of 'Right' and 'Left' in society of the functions of particular institutions.

The genericism of social work reflects the diverse societal origins from which it springs, hence the need for social work to understand its socio-political roots. In this sense social work is as old and as modern as the society in which it has grown. Its problems, inconsistencies, conflicts and strengths can be traced in the history of all societies since the industrial revolution. The role of healer, priest, advocate, interceder, agitator, protector, controller, philanthropist and professional, all have their part in social work, and their origins in history. Which role or combination of roles predominates will depend upon the analysis adopted by social workers. Social work stands at an ideological cross-roads and can no longer afford the luxury of a directionless genericism—if it is to be a radical force then it must choose a radical road.

Table 5.1

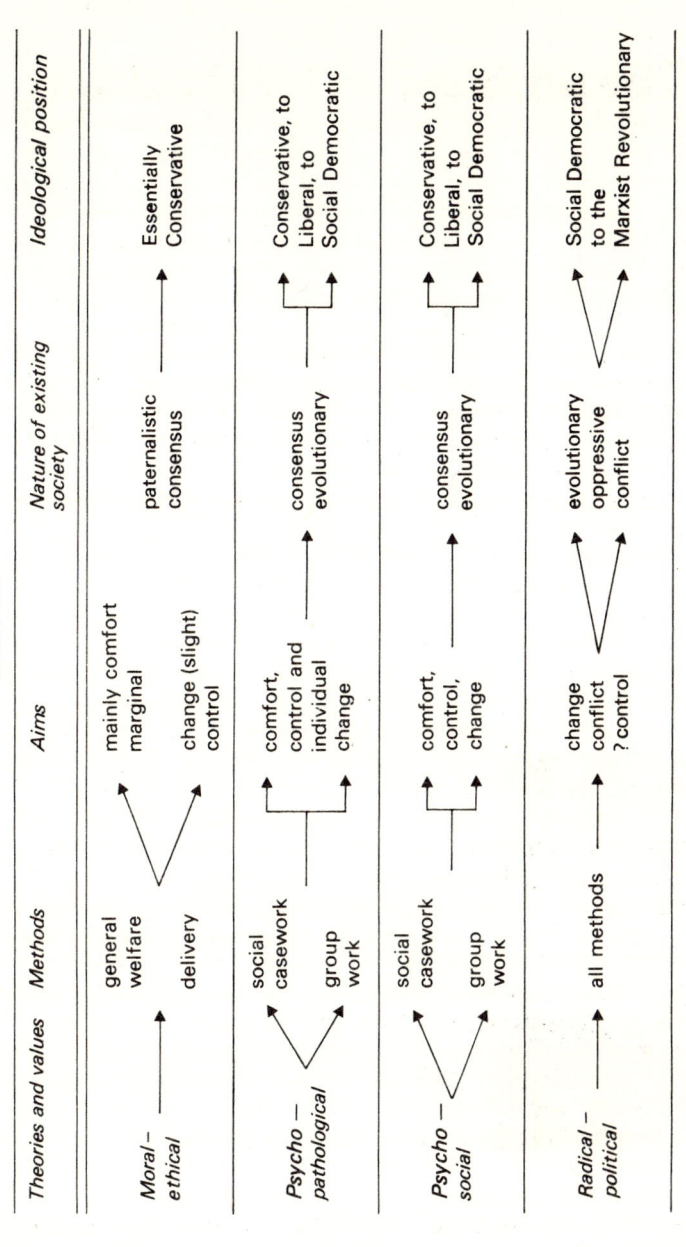

Theories and values	Methods	Aims	Nature of existing society	Ideological position
Moral–ethical	general welfare delivery	mainly comfort marginal change (slight) control	paternalistic consensus	Essentially Conservative
Psycho–pathological	social casework group work	comfort, control and individual change	consensus evolutionary	Conservative, to Liberal, to Social Democratic
Psycho–social	social casework group work	comfort, control, change	consensus evolutionary	Conservative, to Liberal, to Social Democratic
Radical–political	all methods	change conflict ?control	evolutionary oppressive conflict	Social Democratic to the Marxist Revolutionary

Chapter six

The problems of legitimation

We have argued that social work has potential as a radical influence in society. Yet the experience of previous potentially radical professional groups—medicine, education—does not, on the whole, inspire confidence. The tendency has certainly been for such groups to become incorporated into the established institutional structure of an increasingly corporate State. How is social work to avoid a similar fate?

Throughout, we have stressed the need for clear analysis—and nowhere is this more necessary than in this context. To decide upon the future strategy for a radical social work it is essential to have a clear perspective on the existing state of social work *and* on the *potential* of the institutional structure within which social work operates. We would argue that, to a large extent, this analysis must focus upon the problems of 'legitimation'.

What do we mean by 'legitimation' and what relevance has this concept, or cluster of concepts, to our basic theme of the relationships between political culture and social work practice and objectives? At the most basic level we need to understand the ways in which centrally important social institutions and the values propounded or mediated through them are accepted in contemporary society. Why, in other words, are these institutions generally accepted as 'legitimate'? Even more importantly, given our particular focus on social work, to what extent has the criterion for legitimacy changed during the twentieth century? Is society radicalizing its social institutions, and their perceptions, in such a way and at such a pace that radical social change can take place through the agency of legitimate social institutions?

The implicit optimism of this sort of question must be countered by the evident tendency of initially radical institutions to become ever more closely integrated into the established social and ideological structure and thus lose (sometimes partially, often totally) their radicalism.

The relevance for social work in this sort of context is obvious: if, as a radical or potentially radical agency of social change, it can be placed in a proven tradition of reforming social institutions, then its relationship with the established structure need not be a cause for concern. If, alternatively, it can be shown that the existing social and political structure acts in a fundamentally supportive role to a well-entrenched capitalist system, then, for social work to become truly radical, it must question very seriously that relationship. We referred at the end of Chapter 4 to the central importance of the question of 'legitimation'. In that context the crucial question for all those who advocate change, whether they be radical social democrats or Marxist socialists, is to explain why liberal capitalist society is acceptable to the vast majority of people. Why have people, contrary to much socialist prophecy and analysis, come to accept the existing structure? Marxists and social democrats answer this question very differently: for the traditional social democrat the answer lies in the changed nature of capitalist society—the arrival of a 'post-capitalist' system which not only *is* acceptable but *should be* acceptable because of its inherent democracy, and therefore flexibility and potential for further change. Not least amongst these changes has been the creation and consolidation of a whole range of centrally important civil, political and economic freedoms. For the Marxist, however, the fundamentals of capitalist society remain unchanged: it is a society based upon private ownership (the fact that this is increasingly operated through the machinery of a State capitalist system is held not to alter the class nature of the structure). Given this class analysis of social structure, and the Marxist dismissal of social democratic theory as well as action, the reasons for the acceptance of this fundamentally exploitative, irrational and ultimately contradictory, system must lie for the Marxist in the way in which capitalism manages, ideologically, to legitimate its values and institutions.

Whether radical social and political change can come through the existing social and institutional structure lies at the heart of the social democratic argument. But related to this is the equally crucial question of whether a part of the existing structure has in fact developed in implicit opposition to the dominant capitalist ethos. Whether, in fact, capitalism has had to retreat and restructure to such an extent that it has been possible for a sort of socialist fifth-column to establish itself within the infrastructure of capitalist society.[1] If this argument is accepted then the question of the evolutionary potential for radical, socialist change takes on a new significance for both Marxists and social democrats. There is, indeed, a significant number of evolutionary Marxian socialists arguing on precisely this analysis for the creation of a socialist system, not so much through the Labour Party, as through the relatively untainted and indigenous institutions of the working class: most notably the Trade Unions and the Welfare State. The importance of social work as an institutional arena for accomplishing radical change in this latter context, is obvious. Indeed, as Heraud[2] has suggested social work is ideally situated—representing people who are stigmatized by society and presenting values which, although 'officially' sanctioned by that society, are in fact highly critical of its operation. Social work thus stands as advocate for both the alienated and established society—potentially a key agent for evolutionary reform. The emphasis within this radical evolutionary perspective must be upon extra-political movements: if socialism is to be achieved, then across the whole range of social and political life, the radical changes must themselves be genuinely supported and accepted by the mass of the population. The democratic idea underlies this evolutionary perspective: legitimation here is seen as the key criterion for the acceptability of radical change.

We shall thus be examining problems of legitimation and their relation to social work in the following ways. First, an analysis of the traditional liberal, pluralist and social democratic justification for pursuing moderate change through the existing social and political structure. Second, an account of the Marxist critique of this position, which argues that the root cause of the persistence of capitalism lies in the ability of the system to propagate, through the modern institutional complex, values and perspectives supportive to capitalism. Third, we shall look at the arguments underlying the radical evolutionary perspective (embracing some social democrats and some Marxists) which emphasizes the potential for further socialist change within the existing system and stresses the dangers of operating from a more traditional, class-conflict oriented perspective. Finally, we shall attempt to draw some conclusions—in the sense of outlining more clearly, alternative ways of proceeding, particularly in the specifically social work context.

Let us look first at the pluralist and liberal conception of society and the implications that this has for the legitimation question, and more specifically, for social work as an institution operating within this structure. Within this perspective we shall be concentrating mainly on the analysis as it is perceived by social democrats but it is important to emphasize at the outset that, to a large extent, the parameters of this perspective as applied to social work extend from those who believe in the potential for and desirability of *evolutionary* change, whether they be 'Left' social democrats or 'progressive' Conservatives. When we come to analyse the Marxist perspective then this too will include not only those who see social work within an 'orthodox' Marxist analysis but all those who see social work as part of a process whereby the potential for social change must be built up outside the existing social and political institutions and therefore within the extra-parliamentary and *revolutionary* structure.

The central problem of legitimation—of why liberal, capitalist society is acceptable to the vast majority of the population—is, as we have said, of concern to both social democrats and Marxists. There can be little doubt of this general 'acceptance': there have, of course, been notable exceptions in the twentieth-century capitalist society, but generally, since 1945, there has been little State repression in Western Europe and the universal suffrage system has flourished, largely untrammelled, in most Western societies. Left-wing political parties have made relatively little headway in European countries. The Communist parties of France and Italy have indeed become increasingly powerful in the last decade or so and may well exercise power, on a shared basis, in the near future. But this has been achieved by their adopting at least in part a reformist, social democratic stance. And critics, both left and right, argue that the Communist Party has been fundamentally compromised by this revisionism. Either the Communist Party has abandoned its socialism in order to appease the bourgeois system, or its protestations of 'power-sharing' are mere manoeuvring. Whatever the reality behind the rhetoric it is undeniably true that Western European Communism no longer cherishes revolutionary intentions.

As Miliband says,[3] 'The Left, in advanced capitalist countries, has hardly ever, since the First World War, seriously nourished any insurrectionary intention.' Nor is the social, cultural and psychological acceptance of the existing form of society any less evident: despite protestations during the 1960s of alternative cultures in the USA and Europe, the 'Admass' society seems ever more firmly entrenched with the vast majority.[4]

The difference in perspective lies, therefore, not in the definition of the problems but in the nature of the explanation. Do societies, institutions, processes and values become legitimate as a result of a genuinely democratic process that has brought about real and significant change? Popular pressure from an increasingly well-informed and well-educated electorate has resulted, it can be argued, in not only major changes in social, political and ideological structure: it has also produced a consensus of legitimation which underpins all major aspects of our social and political life. Prospects for further change on this pattern are, according to this argument, dependent upon the degree of openness, decentralization and democracy within society generally. Alternatively, Marxists have argued that whilst tremendous social and political changes have taken place over the last century, society remains centrally and crucially capitalist in structure.

The problems of legitimation

As society has, in many ways, become more 'open' and dominated by a more accessible form of capitalist culture, so it has become ever more important for there to be a range of powerful institutions inculcating values supportive to capitalism. We will return to the Marxist argument later but let us first explore further the arguments underlying the social democratic perspective. Most social democrats, certainly most of those in the British Labour Movement, would argue that the open and relatively free society which we enjoy in the twentieth century has come about largely as a result of the struggle of the Labour Movement (i.e. through the Trade Unions and the embryonic political movements) in the late nineteenth and early twentieth centuries. This struggle may well have been aided by a predominantly liberal political culture in the nineteenth century,[5] but the real credit for the creation of our democratic society and its open, accessible and popular institutions lies, so the argument runs, with the mass movement of organized labour who wrested social and political power from an unwilling ruling class in the bitter decades of the late nineteenth century.

Social democrats thus see contemporary social structure as different in kind from the old (and evil) capitalism of the nineteenth century. Arising out of the predominantly élitist but parliamentary traditions of British political culture has developed a genuinely democratic system of government. Central to the whole pluralist perspective of the social democrat is the idea that, ultimately, power resides with the electorate. Since the coming of universal suffrage the central machinery of the parliamentary system of government has been subject to the direct control, through the ballot box, of the popular will. The age-old parliamentary system based upon various élite groups in the eighteenth and nineteenth centuries, has undergone radical changes in the twentieth century and the old structure originally developed to institutionalize ruling-class power now serves an open and democratic structure, where the ordinary citizen has direct and immediate access to his parliamentary representative. Within this democratic, parliamentary system, is it argued, the two major parties, representing distinctive but not totally hostile ideologies,[6] compete for power. The electorate is thus offered at frequent intervals a genuine choice between two identifiable alternatives. Surrounding this fundamentally democratic core structure are various safeguards designed to curb the potentially excessive power of the central executive: thus we have an independent judiciary, a two-chamber legislature (i.e. House of Commons and House of Lords) through which all government legislation has to pass, and a complex system of procedures (committee stages of bills, etc.) designed to modify and qualify government proposals.

The kernel of the political system is thus structured as much as is possible to guarantee the predominance of the 'will of the people'. But, it is argued, modern society has become considerably more complex during the twentieth century and political power has become both more 'diffused' and more 'corporate'. Thus not only has the State become more involved and more powerful across a whole range of issues and areas, corporate pressures have also resulted in the increasing importance of interest or pressure groups in almost all social contexts: and these pressure groups represent a whole range of competing sections and interests in society.[7]

Power in modern societies is diffused and fragmented. Everybody has some power and nobody (and no group) has or can have a monopoly of it. Through the rise of working-class institutions and pressure groups (to say nothing of formal political parties) the protection of the vast majority of the population is assured. (There are, of course, pockets of underprivileged people in society, but these form an ever decreasing minority. A major part of the role ascribed to social work by society is the 'reclamation' and reactivation of these underprivileged minorities: partly because this will benefit those minorities directly, but also because by encouraging such minorities to become integrated, productive sections of society, they will become self-supporting and ultimately supportive contributors to the social system.)

This is the causative, explanatory, framework of the social democrat: a fundamentally evil, hierarchical and unequal society transformed by the efforts of the working class operating within a flexible and liberal political culture. What is the general picture that the social democrat has of contemporary society? The liberal pluralist conception of power distribution in society, to which the social democrat adheres, stresses the diffused nature of power. Not only, as pointed out earlier, is it held that everybody now has a degree of power through organized pressure groups (e.g. Trade Unions)—it is also argued that a whole range of institutions safeguarding democratic rights has now been established: universal suffrage, free and regular elections, representative institutions, citizens' rights (free speech, etc.), protection under an independent judiciary, and a free political culture.

Thus, it is claimed, no government can fail to respond to the wishes of its citizens as expressed through the host of competing 'interest groups' within the political structure. The system is not only responsive to the whole range of interests, it is accessible to most if not all groups and individuals, both via the electoral process and through the operation of pressure groups.

This pluralist view of power structure is rarely held in such extreme or optimistic terms: few serious commentators believe that Western society is *totally* accessible, that there is *total* equality of treatment for *all* interest groups and so on. But, certainly in the USA,[8] many hold that the fundamentals of the democratic structure are solidly in place and that only relatively minor reforms are needed to make them operate effectively. For them this pluralist model of society has nothing to do with 'social democracy' as understood in Western Europe (still less of course with socialism) but stems rather from the liberal-populist tradition of American politics.

For most social democrats in the British context, pluralism is viewed in rather a different light: democratic institutions are seen as creations of the Labour Movement under constant attack, potential if not actual, from the 'forces of reaction'. Nevertheless, the essential point in our context is that the existing system is seen as fundamentally sound, and therefore potentially workable (though of course requiring major reform). Hence it is the duty of all right-thinking people to come to the aid of the organized working-class movement and strive for further reform through the existing structure.

The political strategy for social democrats is clear: in the industrial context 'join your trade union'—in the political, 'join the Labour Party'. But what is the implication for those working in the social work field? First, such an analysis implies an acceptance of the existing network of bureaucratic and political structure. If social work is to become an effective pressure group and institutional force then it must get into the mainstream of the struggle for resources and recognition, and participate in the political complex. Second, it implies that social workers must operate within the norms and practices of existing society. It would not only be dangerous (from a political point of view) to encourage or support social work clients in 'devious' or 'subversive' situations—it would, arguably, be dangerous, even cruel, to encourage clients who are, by definition, vulnerable to take on the 'big battalions'.

To act outside the 'established institutions' would also be quite out of keeping with the acceptance of the social democratic framework: by encouraging, for example, tenants to form themselves into action groups to fight local (often Labour) Councils, social workers would be undermining the potential unity of the working-class movement. More fundamentally, the social democratic social worker would argue that once the primary criterion of the client's welfare, and eventually of his self-determination, is supplanted by a wider collective, or group, criterion, then social work becomes politics (even though the clients may not realize it), and the interests of clients may be subjugated to the assumed interests of the wider collective. Individual clients thus become, social democrats argue, pawns in the Marxist political strategy. In this, as in other spheres, the means-ends dichotomy is of more crucial importance to Marxists than is usually admitted. (The extent to which the short- and mid-term interests of individuals, and whole generations, have been sacrificed to long-term prospects for socialism must disturb even the most determinedly 'structuralist' Marxist.)

The social democratic social worker does indeed see society as potentially legitimate—the potential for reform and evolutionary progress are argued to exist within our present structure. But this does not mean that the social work profession or the individual social worker will no longer have conflicts with his agency. The social worker's role may quite reasonably be one of advocate on behalf of his client against his own authority: there need be no incompatibility provided that both organization and social worker understand the integral political positions they occupy and their ultimate interdependence. For the social democratic social worker this bridging role is crucial as it keeps the individual and 'society' in touch with each other.

The political task is thus to mobilize as much support as possible for the Labour Movement and for social progress amongst and for social work clients. Indeed, according to many social democratic analysts the key to ensuring adequate social and political progress lies in reactivating the dormant interests of the working class *and* in convincing those active outside the Labour Movement to redirect their activities. If social workers—particularly community workers with their range of contacts with the disaffected working class, can convince people of the social democratic position, then an invaluable political function will have been accomplished. Similarly, arguing on Fabian lines, it is a vital part of the educative function to involve both the 'advantaged' and the 'disadvantaged' in an acceptance of the interdependence of different sections of society. The integrative political and social role of social work can thus be seen as a key part of the process whereby social democracy aims to unite rather than divide the social classes.

Another of the strongest arguments of the social democrat has great relevance to the social worker role. Social democrats, particularly those in the old ILP tradition, emphasize the genuinely democratic aspirations of the Labour Movement—the sense in which it represents the freely expressed will of the whole working class.[9] It is this fervent, emotional belief in democratic control which has brought Labour to power and has thus brought social structure to a legitimate position. The strength of the Labour Movement lies, the argument runs, in this close correspondence between the leadership and the mass movement. If this were to be threatened by minority action to achieve political change then the whole basis of democratic control within the movement would be swept away. This is, of course, one of the crucial areas of disagreement between

Communists since Lenin and social democrats. Social democrats have always argued that to take power by force through the agency of a 'professionally' led revolutionary party is fatal because it destroys freedom and endangers the democratic unity of the Labour Movement.

Socialism to the social democrat, and especially to those cast in the ILP mould, is about individual freedom as much as collective ownership,[10] and the whole Leninist idea of a proletarian vanguard is anathema to social democrats on this as on many other counts. Thus, on this argument, if there is to be radical social and political change it must come with the full-hearted consent of the majority of the people and through the relatively democratic institutions of the existing social system. To attempt any extra-parliamentary change would be to endanger all the hard-won democratic freedoms and would result in a totalitarian, authoritarian and repressive regime.

For social workers whose orientation is towards evolutionary change the political role *vis-à-vis* the individual client is also clear. For clients who are seen as actually or potentially 'deviant' or 'disruptive' the social worker's role is fundamentally integrative: helping the 'non-conformist' to cope with conformity—although not necessarily by abandoning his or her nonconformity (an important qualification). The social worker thus acts as a representative—albeit a flexible, liberal and sympathetic representative—of the legitimate institution of a society whose fundamental acceptability acts as the cornerstone assumption of action. The end result of the social worker's intervention should ideally be the reintegration (or at least the reconnection) of the client with society—the precise nature of this reintegration depending upon the individual circumstances.

The degree to which the social worker's analysis of society influences his action will be considerable. For the more conservatively minded social worker the alienated client will be seen as someone who requires reclamation. For the social democratic worker clients are seen to require aid within the system to overcome a situation that threatens to overwhelm them—the social worker's role becomes both to ease the general context of the problem, and more specifically, to enable the client to make his own choices by restoring self-confidence and self-respect.

This is not to say that the social-democratic social worker finds no room for improvement in the existing social system—indeed just as the left-wing Labour MP may find an almost endless list of faults in society, the left-wing social democratic social worker may have many reservations about the system. However, the essential point remains that, because of his analysis, the social democrat holds that the fundamentals of the system *are* relatively accessible, *are* democratic, and *are* therefore capable of radical reform. Such a perspective can only hold that Marxist-inclined community workers trying to organize autonomous and extra-parliamentary activities are, at best, tangential to the primary concerns of social work, and, at worst, are seriously counter-productive.

There are tactical and strategic problems for the left-wing social-democratic social worker who seeks to operate within the system: for the social worker, in other words, who seeks radical political change (see our categories above p. 87) but believes it can and should come about within the existing structure. This is especially a problem for the community worker who, in attempting to radicalize working-class communities, or instil 'deviant' cultural ideas is, from a social democratic perspective, acting in a doubly damaging way: first, it is intrinsically bad, for both the individual client and society, if alienation is heightened and the consciousness of class divisions is increased (the social democratic role should, after all, be the exact reverse of this—integrative and politically constructive); second, the process of radicalization is counter-productive because it detracts from the unity of the Labour Movement (and thus threatens the basis of working-class and social-democratic power: the mass working-class labour organizations, the Trade Unions and the Labour Party). The political task for the social democratic social worker is not to build up alternative organizations to destroy the existing system—it is to strengthen and re-equip the existing organizations to reform society along 'progressive' lines.

The problem of legitimation for the Centre-Right social democrat is, though, more easily soluble. Society *can* be changed: capitalism has retreated under pressure and the potential for progressive change now exists—whether this is seen, as by the Right (e.g. Shirley Williams) in terms of liberal and egalitarian reform or, as by the Left (e.g. Michael Foot) in terms of a partial socialization of the economy, the introduction of other socialist measures, and a refurbishing of the old British Radical tradition. Fundamentally, therefore, the modern capitalist structure *is* legitimate for the social democrat. The 'unacceptable face(s) of capitalism' can and will be eradicated through a consolidation of social democratic power and influence.

Marxists see things somewhat differently.[11] Far from seeing capitalism as fundamentally changed, Marxists maintain that capitalism remains in essence the same exploitative and restrictive structure as in the nineteenth century. Yet there can be no doubt that the crude coercive methods of State and industrial control of the nineteenth century no longer operate;[12] as capitalism has become more sophisticated and as the State has come to play an ever more important role in society so the *ideological* means of control have increased. Marx himself was well aware of the importance of ideology,[13] but with the changing role of the State, the massive increase in importance of State education, the media and many other spheres—the role of ideology in legitimating the existing form of society has become central and crucial. 'The ideas of the ruling class are in every epoch the ruling ideas' (Karl Marx: *The German Ideology*): this has remained the basis of the Marxist explanation of the legitimation question. Later Marxists, in particular Antonio Gramsci, have developed this concept and analysed the role of ideology in terms of 'hegemony'.[14]

This then is the basis of the Marxist answer to the legitimation question: capitalist social structure is legitimated through a whole range of agencies which cultivate acceptance of the ideology of bourgeois society. Thus institutions may be 'accessible'—but the methods of ideological mediation ensure that very few will wish to introduce radically critical opinions. Moreover, by a variety of means, the Left is discriminated against in most contexts.

These are sweeping claims: let us examine them in a little more detail. The ability of Conservatism to survive the transformation of politics from an overtly élitist and aristocratic system to a 'parliamentary democratic' system, has already been noted. Conservatism remains a major ideological and political force in modern society (and this of course applies not only to the UK but throughout the Western world). Conservatism has been *de facto* an important part both of ideological and historical-political developments in the nineteenth and twentieth centuries—and it has also exercised an enormous consolidating and stultifying influence on political culture. Although the Party represents fundamentally the interests of 'big business', its support, electorally and more generally, is by no means confined to the upper echelons of society. Indeed, the British Conservative Party has drawn approximately half its voting strength (at General Elections since 1945) from the working class.[15] In the context of the legitimacy question the key point is the extent to which Conservative ideology, over a broad range rather than on specific policy questions, permeates the mass of the population. Conservatism, as a political movement, has succeeded in dividing the working class: as an ideological force its importance is perhaps even greater. (A simple example of this can be seen in the devotion shown by the great majority of the working class to such a supposedly apolitical and neutral institution as the monarchy).

Whilst large numbers of working-class people support the Conservative Party, and an even larger number are influenced by Conservative ideology, *very* few working-class Conservatives are involved at local, let alone national, level in the Party.[16] Moreover, financial support from business forms the bulk of Conservative

Party financing,[17] and the Conservative Party is intimately connected with and sympathetic to the policies and priorities of 'big business'.[18]

Thus, not only does the Conservative Party stand as the prime upholder of the private enterprise system and command a substantial cross-section of middle- and working-class support, it is also controlled almost exclusively by members of the property-owning class. It thus plays a major role in legitimating the capitalist system to the mass of the population whilst involving a number of those people in either active or passive support for the Party, *and* ensures that control of the Party organization remains in the hands of a small and privileged élite.

If Conservatism is held by Marxists to play a large part in legitimating (and preserving) the capitalist system, the role of social democracy is even more crucial. The British Labour Party was founded with the intention, however hedged around with qualifications and provisos, of substituting socialism for capitalism. This has patently not been achieved (some of the ideological factors involved have already been discussed in Chapter 4), and it has been forcibly argued that the Labour Party has become a 'manager of discontent' within our society rather than a potential vehicle for socialist change.[19]

There are many instances of social democratic parties coming to the rescue of capitalism in crisis—one of the best known being Ramsay MacDonald's formation of the National Government in the 1931 crisis which virtually destroyed the Labour Party during the 1930s. As Ralph Miliband points out, this process cannot be attributed to the personal deficiencies of Labour leaders but must be seen in terms of 'the tremendous weight of conservative pressure upon Labour leaders [also] the ideological defences of these leaders have not generally been of nearly sufficient strength to enable them to resist with any great measure of success conservative pressure, intimidation and enticement.'[20]

All social democratic movements in the West suffer from ideological weakness: a lack of both conviction and depth of analysis which has bedevilled their ability to make political headway in an alien capitalist social and political system. This has applied to the UK more than any other European nation—in part at least because of the paucity of the Marxist tradition within British Socialism. The British Labour Party, at first reformist within the parameters of Fabian socialism, now hardly has pretensions towards a coherent programme of reform. One has only to look at the vacillations, on a virtually day-to-day basis, of the Wilson governments between 1964 and 1970 to appreciate the extent of the lack of direction.[21] It is also instructive in this context to look at Wilson's own accounts of his governmental experience;[22] these display a total disregard for any long-term objectives for British social democracy and concentrate instead upon the minutiae of government life at its most mundane and tedious level.

The Labour Party has long since abandoned the attempt to present forcefully, an alternative ideological perspective. The Party and the Movement have, so Marxists argue, become ever more integrated into the capitalist structure and have used their increasing political, social and industrial power and influence to persuade the working class to bail out capitalism during its periodic crises. The history of the 1964-77 period is remarkable in many ways but not least in the extent to which the representative institutions of Labour (TUC and Labour governments) have taken the initiative in economic and political policy-making and have simultaneously become the front line defenders of capitalism. Tory leaders almost pale into insignificance when set against the successive Wilsonian appeals to the national interest, the Dunkirk spirit, the need for wage 'restraint' (i.e. cuts), public expenditure cuts—and so on. Only the combination of Labour government and TUC could have achieved the relatively passive acceptance of the Social Contract, specifically designed to save the existing system. In this sense social democracy has become an essential and integral part of the mechanism of class control within capitalism, preventing 'irresponsible' outbreaks of class politics on the grounds that these endanger the 'national interest/economy' or whatever.

The extent to which the Labour Movement has lost the missionary zeal of its early years can be judged by the paralysing weakness of the various educational and propagandist outlets of both the industrial and political wings of the organized Labour Movement. All socialist movements are in some senses crusades *against* capitalism and *for* socialism: integral to the whole process of transforming society must be education and discussion, in part to try to instil an alternative socialist consciousness. The creation of opportunity for analysing experience, policies, and so on, in socialist terms must precede any attempts at organized political action. A variety of methods is open to socialist parties: a party newspaper, regular discussion-education groups, encouragement of written material relevant to party interests and so on.

With the exception of its Youth Movement—which has to be purged of Left tendencies at regular intervals[23]—the Labour Party has none of these agencies and shows no desire for them.

For Marxists, then, the Labour Party has lost what little sense of socialist direction and purpose it once had. Its major role lies in legitimating an alien form of society to an increasingly powerful industrial Labour Movement. Whether the Labour and Trade Union movements can be transformed in a socialist direction is, of course, a major issue which we have touched on already and will discuss in more detail later.[24]

The role of the political parties in legitimating the existing system is central—but it is reinforced by numerous other institutions, many of them commonly thought of as apolitical. For example, although there has been, as Miliband has pointed out[25] a 'thin but persistent line of clerics . . . whose hostility to an unjust and "un-Christian" social order has not been set in the comfortable perspective of a timeless gradualism, and whose purpose has often been highly "dysfunctional"', the overall role of the Church has been consistently supportive of the capitalist *status quo*. In the British context this support has included direct and often stressed links between the Established Church and the central institutions of the State: the monarchy, the government and the armed forces. The influence of the Churches has undoubtedly declined in the twentieth century but still exercises a considerable symbolic and underlying influence on large numbers of people who never set foot inside a church.

Just as the established political parties relied to an extent on religious rhetoric in the nineteenth and early twentieth centuries (and this applied as much to the Labour Party's reliance on Methodism and the ideology of Nonconformism as to the Conservatives' connection with the Established Church)—so, in the twentieth century, the political parties have relied upon appeals to nationalism: to the 'national interest' as against 'sectional', 'political', interests.

These appeals, more common, if anything, from *Labour* rather than Conservative governments since 1945, are based upon an implicit and undefined appeal to a higher-order loyalty to the nation 'to which we all belong'—as opposed to the party, or class, or sectional group. The effect of these appeals is to solidify the 'non-political' sectors of the population around the institutions of the State—thus isolating the objectors as 'subversive', 'anti-social', 'unpatriotic' or whatever. (A classic example of this has occurred over the minority of Trade Unionists who have rejected the Trade Union-Labour government 'social contract' and have argued and struck for higher wages, etc.)

A similar ethos of apolitical higher-order loyalty surrounds both the armed forces and the police. As we argued earlier, coercive action to maintain the *status quo* and protect the kernel of capitalism has, largely, given way to more sophisticated means of maintaining control. In the sense of being the instruments of State coercive action, then, the role of the armed forces is, at least for the present, minimal. But there can be little doubt that the armed forces do instil right-wing and clearly anti-socialist ideology in both officers and other ranks: in crisis situations the armed forces could be relied on to take action against any labour 'unruliness' as ordered. More importantly the armed forces have, like most of the other institutions we have mentioned, a firm internal and public image of dependability, acceptability and, above all, of being 'above politics'. They are generally regarded, like the monarchy, as being part of a politically neutral State establishment, and therefore as virtually above question.

If the political role of the armed services is arguably diminishing, that of the police has increased considerably since 1945. Not only are the police devoting more time and thought to crowd control and so on—there is also a strong conviction that it is part of the police function to undermine 'subversive' organizations. The growth of police special powers and the intensification of Special Branch activities have resulted in an increasingly explicit political role for the police as the front-line defence of the State against Left organizations (e.g. the police harassment of the Workers Revolutionary Party Education Centre in 1976). At the same time the police have convinced 'the public' *and themselves* that they are not 'acting politically' in these contexts. To defend the interests of 'the nation', of 'society', against its enemies is not construed as 'political' but as part of that same higher-order apolitical loyalty.[26]

Let us now move on to look, briefly, at the most publicized and vaunted aspects of Western society's 'accessibility' and 'freedom': the media and the education system. Unlike the regimes of the totalitarian Communist bloc, the West is argued, by social democrats as by Conservatives, to enjoy freedom of expression untrammelled by government or State interference. This freedom is by no means wholly illusory (and has been hard fought for over the years) *but* it has to be set, Marxists argue, in the overall context of social and political power. Within the context of contemporary capitalism it becomes apparent that the 'free expression' consists mainly in the propagation of ideas and values that are conducive to the maintenance of the existing system. The overwhelming barrage of pro-capitalist and anti-socialist propaganda coming from the media, and in particular the popular mass appeal media (ITV, the 'popular' press, etc.), masquerades as objective news coverage and thus becomes doubly effective (even Harold Wilson complained of this bias—and he can hardly be termed an extremist). The extent of this pro-capitalist propaganda need not be detailed here but it is perhaps worth noting that this is not merely confined to 'blatant' political postures (e.g. *Daily Telegraph* editorials) or even to universally held prejudices on particular issues (e.g. the paranoiac press hostility to militant Trade Unionism and any brand of socialism to the left of Roy Jenkins); it is evident across the whole range of business public relations and advertising. Not only does the image of the 'soulful corporation' caring for the consumer come through the public relations machines of big business—the persistent concentration upon 'socially approved values and norms: integrity, reliability, security, parental love, childlike innocence, neighbourliness, sociability, etc.'[27] as identifiable with private enterprise in the common desire for a better society is the underlying theme of almost all business self-presentation. The rationale of business—to make profits—enters the picture only in as much as 'making profits' is held to be a quasi-altruistic exercise designed to maintain full employment, prosperity and general social welfare. The operations of 'business' under free enterprise are thus continually presented, through the media as well as through the public relations machine of industry itself, as legitimate, and altruistic, quite unrelated to 'politics' or 'ideology'. This whole 'common sense', 'national interest' approach dovetails neatly with the political parties' orientations as described earlier.

The organs of the media themselves are, of course, almost totally dominated by supporters, indeed major shareholders, of the existing capitalist system. This is not to deny the existence, and the vital importance, of the minority press espousing the whole range of alternative ideology; nor to ignore the important 'minority interest' coverage on radio and TV. But as far as the *mass* audience newspapers and TV channels go the parameters of opinion expressed are contained well within the assumptions underlying the capitalist system. Thus, for example, there is in the UK a fair degree of impartiality shown between Conservative, Labour and Liberal Parties, but any views falling outside this perspective are usually dismissed as undesirable, subversive, or just 'cranky'. Nor should this surprise us: the ownership of the media industry is staggeringly restricted and the degree of control exercised by those working within the media, minimal.[28] The media may in principle be accessible—and in theory objective: in reality they are to a greater or lesser degree closed to any views falling outside the narrow consensus and dismissive of any perspective which threatens the received interpretations of reality.

Finally, in this by no means exhaustive list of social institutions held by Marxists to inculcate the dominant ideology and thus acceptance of the existing form of society, let us look briefly at the education system. Again, this is held up by defenders of Western society as evidence of the very real differences between the totalitarian indoctrination process masquerading as education in the Communist world, and the genuinely open-ended and flexible education system of societies such as exist in Britain. Education in our society is held to be quite apart from 'politics'.

Yet the education system is, arguably, the most important

institution of all in ensuring that the capitalist system is accepted by each new generation. Far more than in the past socialization occurs through the education system. Not only are the future ruling class trained through the public school system for 'leadership', and instilled with an explicitly Conservative ideology of hierarchy, tradition and the rest, they also continue to have access to far more educational facilities than State schools and a closer relationship with the older universities. Much more important than the training and conditioning of the ruling class through the public school system, however, is the 'class confirming' role performed by the State education system. The economic (and social) function of the education system is to provide the requisite number of skilled and unskilled workers to meet industrial requirements: as capitalist industrialists never tire of telling us there is little 'use' in having 'too many' graduates in Arts or other 'impractical' fields. The basic function of education under capitalism is to produce young adults of an appropriate educational level to meet industrial needs: the rest is merely icing on the cake. If education is seen in this utilitarian, functional way then, obviously, it is essential that, for the vast majority, the secondary system should confirm their working-class social position and condition them to accept a semi-skilled or unskilled job. As Miliband points out the net effect of this is to produce the belief that 'they are the prisoners, not of a social system, but of an ineluctable fate.'[29] Over and above this class-confirming role the education system is overwhelmingly dominated by, usually implicit, bourgeois values. The ethos of the school, even in predominantly working-class areas, is solidly bourgeois in orientation and specifically aimed, through the hierarchical structure of the school and the ideological content of the teaching, at producing a broadly conformist perspective. Reform in education has come a long way since the 1944 Butler Act—the measures of the 1974 Labour government to introduce a comprehensive system being merely the latest in a series of mildly egalitarian measures. For socialists of any hue educational reform still has a very long way to go and for most Marxists education *per se* cannot offer the key to fundamental social and political change, conditioned and structured as it is by the capitalist societal context in which it operates.

This catalogue of legitimating forces is not intended to be comprehensive, nor has the detailed evidence available been presented. Our intention here is rather to point out how, on the Marxist analysis, most of the major social and political institutions, usually thought of as guardians of freedom, objectivity and democracy, are in fact very effective mediators of bourgeois ideology. Again, it is important to stress that the inculcation of this ideology is by no means total and that, more often than not, the process is not conscious. This, of course, makes for a far more effective means of legitimation than overt coercive methods of social control. The net effect, according to Marxist analysis, is to create an almost impregnable ideological structure which reinforces repeatedly the legitimation of the capitalist system.

And yet there *are* insoluble contradictions within the social and economic structure of capitalism and as these manifest themselves in a whole variety of areas, conflict becomes more and more widespread. For the Marxist the key problem in the contemporary context is to develop political consciousness to a level where the working class and its allies can develop socialist politics and strategy from the recurring crises of capitalism. As these crises deepen, and as the Labour Movement becomes ever stronger industrially, the central problem remains as Lenin characterized it: to transform Trade Union consciousness into political consciousness. Whether the Labour Party is the potential vehicle for such a transformation has already been discussed—and must remain a focal point for further discussion. But, equally important, bearing in mind the crucial legitimating role played by other social and political institutions, is the inherent potential of such institutions in contexts other than the organized Labour Movement.

In our context the crucial questions for the Marxist social worker must be, first, whether social work is a potential vehicle for achieving a heightened socialist consciousness, and second, if it has this potential, how it can be fulfilled. Others on the Left have argued, though, that this radicalizing role is best fulfilled not through the heightening of conflict-oriented class consciousness and the consequent construction of alternative vehicles for socialist transformation, but rather through the adaptation of existing institutions and organizations. By further pressurizing the potentially socialist aspects of existing structures, it is argued, the system can be radicalized through mass, democratic pressure. This view certainly rejects the pluralist assumptions: the unacceptable nature of existing social structure is not disputed—and the need for radical change is as strongly held as it is by 'orthodox Marxists'. It is the *means* of achieving this change that sharply differentiates these perspectives. The rationale of this approach is based both upon specific social analysis and upon wider political considerations. On the wider political front it can be argued that, whereas it may have been reasonable for Marx to talk prescriptively about the need for decades of civil war, following the clash of social classes, in order to establish a socialist system—to advocate violent conflict in the nuclear age is both irresponsible and unrealistic in socialist terms. Future conflict could not be confined to nationally based conflict but would inevitably involve intervention by the major power blocs. With the proliferation of nuclear weapons amongst some of the middle-range powers the dangers of a nuclear holocaust become even greater. There is thus a need for humanity as a whole to acknowledge its ability, technologically, to self-destruct. Once this has been accepted, the context of the argument for social change is drastically revised: at its extreme, the possibility of massive human annihilation through nuclear conflict may be precipitated by major class conflict. Can Marxists therefore *afford* to advocate violent revolution in the nuclear age? Such speculations may at first sight seem far removed from the tasks facing social work. But if, as we have argued, the political choice between 'evolutionary' and 'revolutionary' perspectives for social change is highly relevant to social work concerns then the implications of the means of achieving these objectives must also be of direct concern to social workers as to all others involved in 'politically sensitive' areas.

The force of this argument cannot be denied—but how precisely do those advocates of evolutionary radicalism justify their claims that the existing structure has 'socialist potential'? One of the most convincing exponents, from a Marxist viewpoint, of this view is Michael Barratt-Brown.[30] Starting from the argument that the State must be seen as in some respects 'independent from and superior to all social classes, as being the dominant force in society rather than the instrument of a dominant class',[31] Barratt-Brown argues that only when the working class is totally excluded from involvement in State institutions can the State structure be seen as a monolith which can be toppled only by organized violent action from outside the system. In our contemporary context, he argues, 'the State is not a monolith but made up of a set of institutions designed to incorporate the class struggle, and working-class organizations thus develop a dual role of acting within the State system as well as acting to replace it.'[32] The task for the working-class movement is thus to gain an ever-increasing control in the various institutions of the State and by capturing State power through evolutionary pressure, move eventually to a position where the attainment of a fully socialist system becomes possible.

Under this perspective what areas of the existing institutional complex can be argued to contain evidence, actual or potential, of the socialist orientations of the structure? Basically, Barratt-Brown claims, the increasing role of the State has resulted in the creation of a whole new stratum of employment, involvement *and* ideology. It may well be true that the 'destabilizing and polarizing effects of private capital accumulation'[33] form the basis for the vast increase in State intervention in the economy (rising rapidly since the 1940s to a percentage of GNP now well over 50 per cent). But the *form* that that intervention has taken has been largely the result of public demand, predominantly from the Labour Movement, for publicly provided social services.

The importance of this concentration of national resources, via the State, in the broad field of social services has, it is argued, two very important aspects. First, the fact that over 2·5 million 'medical, educational and social workers plus another million of the lower echelon of local and national government officers'[34] are now organized and largely TUC affiliated, indicates the arrival of a powerful 'institutional' occupational group with a strong and direct interest in the *concept* and *structure* of a socially-oriented society. Second, the ideological criteria of the Welfare State system— including the social work profession— arguably operate from bases different from those of capitalism. Both the motivation and the practices of the Welfare State services are claimed[35] to introduce socialist values into the central structures of capitalism. Both the legality of Trade Unions and the rapid extension of welfare services are thus held to demonstrate the growing power of working-class and socialist ideas within the State. Welfare services are based on the principle of free treatment 'provided purely on the basis of *need* and not of cash payment'. (Similarly, Trade Unions can be seen as working-class organizations based upon fellowship, unity, co-operation and so on in explicit value opposition to the private enterprise institutions that they oppose.)

The task for those who accept this perspective is thus to extend and fortify the working-class and socialist incursions into capitalism. Far from creating alternative structures to challenge the power of the State (and of the capitalist class) the Labour Movement *and* the existing socialistically inclined institutions in society, should continue to pressurize for further progress towards a fully socialized and socialist system.

The success of this pressure will depend to a large extent on the degree to which mass support can be mobilized. Whereas the 'orthodox Marxist' hopes to create alternative structures (or develop the existing integrative organizations, such as the Trade Unions, into overtly oppositional forces), the perspective we have been discussing stresses the importance of simultaneously radicalizing and making legitimate to the mass, the potentially socialist institutions of the modern State. Thus, for example, by radicalizing the structure of power within the Welfare State system, and within the industrial system by means of increased participation, decentralization and democratization, it becomes possible both to increase the socialist nature of the institutions and to broaden the base of mass support for this radicalization.

The 'orthodox Marxist' runs the risk, if not the certainty, so the argument runs, of creating through social conflict an authoritarian and undemocratic system whereby the gains of a new and more socialist social order are more than counterbalanced by at best a severe restriction of civil freedoms and at worst wholesale purges and imprisonment. The key to the avoidance of this situation is to pressurize *with mass support* for the extension of those aspects of the system which are already heavily influenced with working-class and socialist ideas: in other words to legitimate radicalism.

The emphasis is thus very much upon the potential of institutions not directly concerned with the central political enterprise but rather with the corporate institutions of modern society.

For radical social workers the implications are clear. If society is capable of evolutionary progress to a socialist structure, and if this process is centrally dependent upon the already powerful institutions which have been established on socialist assumptions, then social workers must aim to reintegrate their clients into society whilst at the same time convincing them of the potential available for humane *and* radical change in institutional terms. In as much as social work is a key sector within the Welfare State structure, and an even more important influence on Welfare State *ideology*, then it should have a central role in its own right as a catalyst for the dual role of legitimating and radicalizing social change.

As we argued at the beginning of this chapter the view taken of 'legitimation' will depend on overall ideological orientation. The majority of social workers have either a conservative or mainstream social democratic ideology, whether explicit or implicit. For this majority group the broad pluralist framework, in as much as questions of legitimation are of concern to them, will predominate. In our view this explanation of society, and, consequently the prognosis as to social work roles, is a false one and its acceptance by the large majority of people within Western society can be explained only in terms of the various processes of legitimating agencies that we described briefly above (and which are discussed in much more detail in Ralph Miliband's *The State in Capitalist Society*).

From this radical viewpoint the central question becomes whether we can either envisage or support potentially violent means of overturning such a system—by for example the creation of alternative, class-conflict oriented structures specifically intent upon challenging directly for State power. It may be that for socialists there is no alternative but to work for the creation of such a revolutionary movement—despite the dangers of wider conflict and possible self-destruction which are so frighteningly inherent in such a process. If this is so then social workers whose ideological framework can be broadly characterized as Marxist will have clear responsibilities to play their part in the creation of an alternative consciousness and range of institutions to give expression to genuinely socialist aspirations. Social work in this context occupies a crucial bridging area between the radical intellectual Left and the most obviously exploited sections of the working class—and this is most dramatically demonstrated in the situation of the Marxist community worker.

From this perspective the role of the social worker is generally to raise socialist political consciousness, as we have argued earlier. But a crucial part of this process is to undermine the acceptance of, and often support for, the legitimating institutions of society. The social worker thus uses his professional role, to expose the very system of which his profession is, at present, a part: a dangerous but not altogether ignoble role!

Alternatively, and perhaps for the socialist more optimistically, if the existing structure has within it already extant considerable areas of working-class power whose socialist values are increasingly put into operation, then, despite the stultifying effects of the agencies of legitimation, it is possible to push forward *through existing channels* to a socialist transformation. The role of the social worker in this context is to be both radical *and* integrative, to ensure that mass support can be given to radicalization proposals which can then be carried through democratically and without need to resort to authoritarian control.

The key problem, in this debate on the Left, obviously lies in whether or not agencies such as the Welfare State (and the Trade Unions) really have the radical potential that is claimed for them. How far, in reality, can social work claim to be part of a wider Welfare State structure that is in its present form moving towards an evolutionary but radical socialist transformation? And how do these *social* movements find *political* expression?

This lies at the heart of the radical dilemma in relation to the legitimation debate. Accepting the supportive legitimizing role of most major social institutions to capitalism, the 'way forward' for radical social workers depends upon their analysis of the contemporary role of, first, the political and industrial Labour Movement, and second, the institutions of the modern State.

It is to further discussion of these questions, amongst others, that we turn in the final chapter.

Chapter seven

Reform, revolution, or...?

By now it will have become clear that the authors, though both socialists, have differing perspectives on analysis and prescription. The main purpose of this final chapter is to explore in more detail the differences between the evolutionary 'democratic socialist' and revolutionary Marxist perspectives, both in general terms and in the specific context of social work.

Throughout the book we have argued that social work is political—at the most obvious level in its relationship to its political masters—local and central government. As Titmuss[1] and Pinker[2] have pointed out, questions of resource allocation, which are of central concern to Welfare Services including social work, are ultimately questions of political priorities. Even more importantly, we have argued that all social work perspectives stem from and are deeply influenced by an ideological framework: the 'apolitical' perspective, because it assumes a static and acceptable social structure, is inherently a conservative stance. But, before we begin the discussion over *socialist* perspectives, we must briefly explain our rejection of the conservative framework. We would both hold generally to the Marxist critique of Conservatism (see Chapter 3) which sees both the Party and the ideology as supporting the existing fundamentally barren and obsolescent capitalist system. Conservatism on this view is thus reactionary, in both senses, and is identified with the preservation of an irrational, immoral and ultimately self-destructive social, economic and political structure which can no longer fulfil the developmental aspirations of mankind.

Change is not only necessary but inevitable:[3] and change in the world and our society is taking place at an unprecedented rate. Any society which fails to adapt is heading for destruction. To come to terms with the need for change (and to decide on the appropriate way to implement necessary changes) is a major task, and one in which the welfare professions, among them social workers, have a part to play. (Indeed it has been argued [Chapter 2] that the creation of social work was given impetus, in part, by this need for change.) This demands the highest attributes of the professional—informed, detached, non-exploitative, rational judgment, free of personal bias and prejudice.[4] But professionalism alone cannot resolve social workers' problems, let alone society's: there must be a sense of direction and ideological commitment—in our view a social, and a socialist, purpose. Our title of 'Reform, revolution, or? . . .' suggests the choices open, but leaves the third alternative 'Repression', unstated. Orwellian predictions of a totalitarian world of double-think where freedom, justice and civilization have all but disappeared, no longer seem far-fetched. Despite material advances, the values and structures of capitalism have proved incapable of reversing the discernible and undeniably suicidal trends in world society. The briefest look at the history of our own century reveals a cynicism, and a reckless disregard for humanity, by almost all societies' leaders: the First World War and the subsequent Versailles settlement, the Nazi-Soviet pact, Hiroshima, Suez, 'Vietnam, Hungary, Czechoslovakia, and the contemporary horrors of racist and totalitarian regimes the world over—the roll-call is one of unmitigated disaster and folly, applying to both Western and Eastern power blocs. Not only does this irrational and obscene system manifest itself in times of crisis: the horrific waste, both human and material, surrounds us all the time.

It is a revulsion against this ludicrous but deadly pattern of behaviour that has impelled people to involve themselves in occupations and campaigns that seem to have some direct humanitarian and social pay-off. Social work is one such major area. But if it is to achieve anything other than a transitory success it must be motivated both by a desire to achieve socialist, environmental change *and* by an understanding of the forces that have brought our society to its present position.[5]

For socialists the issue is stark: annihilation, or at best authoritarian repression, or the achievement of a truly liberated and egalitarian socialist system. On this the authors are agreed, although differing on both analysis and prescription.

R.T. We might start by outlining the major areas of agreement and disagreement in broad analytical terms and then relate these arguments to the present and future position of social work.

C.P. There are of course many areas of agreement between the 'democratic socialist' and Marxist positions and these are illustrated when we come to discuss the specific functions of social work. It might be helpful however at this point to clarify what I mean by the 'democratic socialist' concept: perhaps the easiest way to do this would be to quote from Aneurin Bevan, who in his person and career epitomized what is best in this position. He wrote in 1952:[6]

> The philosophy of democratic socialism is essentially cool in temper. It sees society in its context with nature and is conscious of the limitations imposed by physical conditions. It sees the individual in his context with society and is therefore compassionate and tolerant. Because it knows that all political action must be a choice between a number of alternatives it eschews all absolute prescriptions and final decisions. Consequently, it is not able to offer the thrill of the complete abandonment of private judgment, which is the allure of Soviet Communism and of Fascism, its running mate. Nor can it escape the burden of social choice so attractively suggested by those who believe in the principles of *laissez-faire* and in the automatism of the price system. It accepts the obligation to choose among different kinds of social action and in doing so bears the pain of rejecting what is not practicable or less desirable.
>
> Democratic socialism is a child of modern society and so of relativist philosophy. It seeks the truth in any given situation, knowing all the time that if this is pushed too far it falls into error. It struggles against the evils that flow from private property, yet realizes that all forms of private property are not necessarily evil. Its chief enemy is vacillation for it must achieve passion in action in the pursuit of qualified judgments. It must know how to enjoy the struggle, whilst recognizing that progress is not the elimination of struggle but rather a change in its terms.

Stirring words? I should point out, however, that I am not attempting to offer a tactical consideration of how the social worker should tackle his day-to-day tasks but rather seeking to outline an overall strategy of which social work is but a part. There is a need to concentrate upon *ends*, as well as means. The danger is, of course, that 'reform' may develop through 'stumbling incrementalism'[7] which many fear will lead nowhere. Yet by following a 'purist' dogma or party the activist may render himself politically and socially impotent—being left with little but a spotless ideological soul. It is puerile not to be involved because the possible victory is only partial or even marginal.

R.T. The quotation from Bevan usefully demonstrates one of the differences between our positions: the spirit of this definition is highly pragmatic whilst maintaining a moral criterion for action. No doubt this is the unfortunate result of many years' entanglement in the Labour political machine: but the overriding implication of compromise, of regretful adjustment to the 'limitations imposed by the physical conditions' is at the heart of British Labourism's absorption into the existing socio-political structure. The (vague) moral commitment is there but there is no hard analysis, largely, one suspects, because of the unpleasant political actions which would then be required. For the Marxist, the central business of politics resides in the class conflict that is endemic to capitalism: the rejection or avoidance of this basic socialist tenet by the Labour Left has rendered it largely ineffectual, or, as in Bevan's case, led to specific and explicit collaboration with the right-wing leadership.

Perhaps we can return to questions of how best to achieve socialist change. At this stage I would like to outline some aspects of the broad Marxist analysis of capitalist society which we might agree about. We both reject the Crosland-Gaitskell[8] thesis that we now live in a post-capitalist society, where the task of the Labour Movement is merely to introduce humane and egalitarian reform. There are structural tensions and contradictions within the present capitalist system which cannot be eradicated by piecemeal reform, or indeed by social or governmental action *unless* this is allied to a clear commitment to restructure society along socialist lines.

Whilst these contradictions are largely economic[9]—that is, related to the capitalist system of economic organization and the consequent property relations—there is a whole range of important social and political problems endemic to capitalism. As Marx predicted, the increasing concentration, centralization and monopolization of economic power has resulted in a heightening of class consciousness on the part of the working class. The size and social importance of the Trade Unions in Britain, as in other Western societies, has increased tremendously during the twentieth century: as the ownership of the productive process becomes ever more concentrated, the system becomes ever more social in nature. Contrary to the expectations of social democratic analysts of the 1950s, the increasing proportion of white-collar workers has resulted in the 'unionization' of large sections of workers, hitherto regarded as 'middle-class' by themselves and others.[10]

C.P. This is an interesting development, both psychologically and socially, but it was the Labour Movement that brought these disparate groups together and it is the Labour Movement which gives expression to the aspirations of ordinary people for a more just and humane form of society. This shows a potential for further developments which might unite the previously overtly opposed socio-economic groups by demonstrating each to the other that they have many areas of mutual interest and that so often both are equal victims of an irrational and humanly wasteful economic system.

One point worthy of particular note is that, although power has become further concentrated, the Trade Unions themselves have become part of the institutional framework of capitalism, thus enabling the organized working class to influence, perhaps decisively, the way in which capitalism operates.

As we have already said, I do not dispute the basic analysis and criticism: capitalism *is* an irrational economic system and it *has* produced class conflict. But it has become far more flexible and has been more drastically reformed than the nineteenth-century socialists could have imagined.

There are several other related points of criticism of the Marxist analysis that might be appropriately discussed here. Despite its considerable merits, Marxist analysis seems to me to have three main areas of weakness: a neglect of the psychological aspects of 'human nature'; the rigidity and restriction of Marxist 'historical materialism'; and the inability of the Marxist framework to adequately synthesize past and present to *create* a contemporary socialist society (or indeed a cohesive and genuinely socialist party).[11]

Psychologically Marxists have been, implicitly, far too optimistic about 'human nature'. 'Change the environment and you change the man'—this seems to have been the Marxist creed. And yet Marx himself—undoubtedly an intellectual giant, possessing an amazingly powerful moral driving force allied to analytical genius—was a man of his time! Marx was a German nationalist, who considered Central European nationals as virtual *Untermenschen*—and he had a disdainful, insensitive attitude to the 'undeserving poor', the lumpenproletariat.[12] If a man of his genius and commitment can hold such attitudes in his personal life, what hope is there that lesser folk can be freed from their prejudices and self-seeking natures within one lifetime?

It might be thought to be naïve to quibble at the 'personal' lives of Marxists as if they in their persons epitomized the theory—yet the practical test of the kind of commitment you envisage would require a large number of comfortable, middle-class activists (some of them with university jobs!) to give up their status and security and 'join the people'. Yet there are still, after all, more Marxists in Hampstead than Hartlepool . . .!

In historical terms Marxists have stuck too rigidly to the categories and concepts of the nineteenth century. Maybe the really powerful forces in society no longer reflect the labels of 'capital' and 'labour' as separate entities (and indeed political divisions have often lagged behind 'objective' structural changes);[13] after all, capitalism has changed tremendously since Marx's time. The working class in particular has made great material and political advances, and the polarization of classes and the immiseration of the working class which Marx predicted, has not taken place: quite the opposite in fact. Even in the unlikely event of Marx's predictions of imminent collapse being correct, there is little that either individuals or organizations can do to alter the 'inevitable' course of history: in the meantime, it seems reasonable to improve and reform where we can.

Finally, Marxists, and especially Marx himself, have always been rather coy about the relationship between the interregnum of proletarian dictatorship and the final, total freedom of a truly communist society. If bureaucracy is inimical to socialism and if the State is to 'wither away', how is this process of necessary change to be accomplished? Marx implied that the socialist consciousness established through revolutionary struggle would enable a unified and expanding workers' movement to build a new society. Yet at the same time he also recognized that this new world would 'in every respect, economically, morally and intellectually be stamped with the birthmarks of the old society from whose womb it emerges'.[14] This comment was more prescient than perhaps Marx realized: the historical reality of the twentieth century has seen every attempt at building a Marxist society bedevilled by a highly centralized, bureaucratized Communist Party rule. This is hardly surprising: the people who create the revolution have themselves been socialized under the 'old order' and cannot be expected to change their nature overnight. When societies are under major stress, as in the aftermath of a wartime defeat for example, a popularly supported brief revolution may well be possible[15]—but a peacetime, 'guided', revolution creating a new and truly democratic social structure has yet to be realized.

The twin themes of Marxian prescription for a socialist society—the creation of a genuine workers' democracy, operating through a decentralized institutional structure, and the rational planning of such a society via an ideologically committed vehicle such as the Communist Party—are quite incompatible.

R.T. To take your arguments in order, I think you make a number of false assumptions in your 'psychological' criticism. Certainly Marx was a 'man of his time' and as such had some social attitudes (male chauvinism, and nationalist prejudices for example) which seem strikingly unsocialist—as viewed of course from a late *twentieth-century* perspective. But Marxism does not begin and end with Marx—it is a living, dynamic framework of analysis: to regard it as static, 'revealed truth' is a profoundly *unmarxist* attitude. Nothing is, or can be, given—after all, Marx's favourite motto was 'doubt everything'! Marxism has developed in the twentieth century and the fact that racial prejudice *et al.* are now disappearing from the socialist movement is an encouraging indication of the ideological development since Marx's time. Equally important in this 'psychological' context is the crucial need for the development of an alternative socialist consciousness. Only with a clearly and deeply held socialist perspective can there be any hope of socialist achievement. It is capitalist ideology that requires change, not 'human nature', for it is that ideology that in our mass society informs all social and political thought and action. There is nothing inherent in man's 'psychological' nature which prohibits the achievement of a socialist system—in fact, as 'civilization' develops, the potential for socialist change at this psychological level increases also. Individuals will always have weaknesses and strengths—psychological or otherwise. It is one of the tasks of the collective, mutually supportive socialist movement to imbue a general ethos of socialist ideals and eradicate, rationally, anti-socialist attitudes (such as racial prejudice).

Your second point concerning the rigidity of Marxian historical analysis is impossible to answer briefly. Fundamentally, you have not presented either Marx or later Marxist analysis correctly. Marx never claimed that there were only two classes: he predicted that as capitalist society developed two classes would emerge as the most important protagonists in the class struggle. History has certainly justified this prediction—although later Marxists have argued that he grossly underestimated the adaptability of capitalism to adjust both structurally and institutionally to an ever-growing working-class movement.[16] Even more important, I think it can be conclusively shown that although capitalism has changed since the nineteenth century, the fundamental structure of the *system* remains wholly capitalist in nature. In this context we will have to leave this as mere assertion—but the case has been fully argued in the British context by a whole range of writers on the New Left in the 1960s and 1970s.[17] Class divisions, and thus power and wealth distribution, *do* correspond strikingly to the Marxist framework of class structure. And the tremendous power of the modern, centralized, corporate State has massively increased the structural (i.e. economic, industrial and social) and ideological control of capitalism. It therefore seems to me that you are quite straightforwardly mistaken!

Incidentally, Marx never claimed 'historical inevitability': at the heart of the Marxist system of analysis is the dual process of *objective* historical development which determines the possibilities of action, and *subjective* political action, which determines the actual pattern of historical events. The intervention of socialist ideology and socialist organization is absolutely essential to achieve a socialist society.

I am more sympathetic to your third point: that in practice Marxism, so far, has resulted in near total bureaucratization (as in Soviet Russia) and this of course cannot be defended. The fault though does not seem to me to be one of the theory but of practical socialist ideology and organization. The extent of bureaucratization will depend upon the determination and commitment of the socialist movement and the individuals within it. With all the necessary qualifications about the Russian Revolution, and Lenin and Trotsky's development of Marxist thought, it would be hard to accuse either man, or the party at the time of their prominence, of bureaucratization. As I say, your point seems to me valid, but is soluble given sufficient determination and socialist commitment.

C.P. We have obviously reached a point where, on some aspects, we differ fundamentally. I would like to return to some of the immediate 'practical' issues. Even if Marxian analysis is, in the broadest terms, accurate, the *prescription* for creating a socialist society offered by Marx is still simplistic and gravely deficient. For example, as Michael Foot points out, while the Marxist theory of the State is inescapable, the desired socialist State structure leaves too many valid and central liberal questions unanswered.

'Somehow a synthesis must be devised. What adequate checks could there be on exorbitant power but thriving democratic institutions? And if they could be used to secure fundamental changes by persuasion instead of force and bloodshed, how much more beneficial and enduring the victory could be.'[18] Democratic socialists believe that socialist change can only come through evolutionary *democratic* processes, to achieve any *practical* benefits; and in practice, despite the value of Marxian *criticism*, there is little evidence to suggest that Marxists have been any more successful than others in building the 'good society'.

The Labour Movement in Britain has achieved a great deal, not only in improving living standards and conditions of work, but in the realm of civic freedoms and political democracy. Comparing the 1970s with the 1870s quickly shows the extent of the progress: universal suffrage; free elections; freedom of speech and assembly; and freedom of the press—an impressive list. There are of course deficiencies in the overall picture, but the essential point for the democratic socialist is the extent to which society has moved over the last hundred years—progressive achievement that the early socialists would have considered almost millennial.[19] Further reform of capitalism is possible—through a whole range of progressive social institutions, including an aware and radicalized, humanitarian social work.

Marx not surprisingly failed to foresee the flexibility of capitalism's response to the increasing power of the working-class movement: not only has the power balance shifted, the State has become supremely important in almost every aspect of social structure, and despite its limitations, the State is influenced by some democratic controls. It is in this context that we must look at social work.

It is usually assumed that Marx had little confidence in the ability of piecemeal social reform to transform a capitalist into a socialist system. However, some of the earliest aspects of 'welfare' legislation in the nineteenth century—the Factory Acts, the Ten Hours Act—were closely studied by Marx, who was greatly encouraged by the legal recognition of the workers' 'rights' and the slow but sure restrictions imposed by the State upon private employers. As Marx said, 'This was not only a great political success, it was the victory of a principle.'[20]

In an interesting article[21] Mishra argues that Marx was indeed interested in the potential for reform through welfare legislation. Marx and Engels are, it is argued, stating a fundamental welfare criterion for the future Communist society in their famous formulation 'to each according to his needs'.[22] If 'absolute welfare' is taken as the objective of Communist society then there is a continuum, progressing from the 'low' of a 'perfect competition' capitalist society, ruled by the cash nexus where the individual's social definition is seen purely in terms of the economic worth of his labour power; through an evolutionary process of welfare development as society comes to see the individual and collective social needs in terms of a more rounded humanist approach. Eventually a welfare-oriented Communist society will be attained.

On this argument Marx's system of development can thus be seen as clearly evolutionary and centrally dependent upon welfare reform. This is not to claim that Marx was a 'reformist' rather than a 'revolutionary': but he did admit the *possibility* of a peaceful transformation to Socialism in England[23] and he did recommend to continental socialists that they study some of the 'sanitary' reforms and British Parliamentary blue books.[24] For the democratic socialist there is, as Mishra argues, a strong case for thinking that piecemeal changes 'could be milestones in the movement of capitalist society towards a different social order', and it is in this positive context that I would wish to consider the potential of social reform through social work.

There are two practical aspects here—social work must operate at two levels, at the 'subliminal', or unconscious level, and at the rational, conscious level. By 'subliminal' I mean those aspects of individual and societal life which are unconscious, not so much in the classic Freudian sense, but more in the sense of the irrationality of unconscious prejudice. Social workers, via their education in the socio-behavioural sciences, are well placed to understand these forces, which in all probability the individual would disown but which can all too easily be activated if conditions arise which favour the development of such 'primitive responses'. (Typical examples are the hostility expressed about racial and sexual minorities.[25])

At the overt, rational level social work has a professional duty to influence policy and legislation in a progressive and radical direction, utilizing its favourable strategic position of being a bridge between the majority of society and its 'deviants' (however labelled or categorized). Both tasks are ideological—but both also involve a complex and sophisticated professionalism.

R.T. There seem to be two central points here: the potential, in terms of socialist change, of welfare reforms, and the role of the State. On the first point, I agree that piecemeal welfare reforms can be important—both in terms of individual and collective alleviation of suffering and in terms of 'strategic' Labour Movement demands. Marx certainly saw the gains made by the embryonic Labour Movement in Britain in the nineteenth century as being crucial in establishing a powerful base from which the industrial, Trade Union struggle could be translated into political action. The *crucial* point, though, is that the general burden of Marx's (and later Marxists') prognosis held that pressure for further progressive social and political reform would lead to the establishment of an increasingly powerful and ambitious Labour Movement—which would in turn lead to more extremist demands for reform, and so on. Eventually, the situation would be reached where the existing capitalist system could no longer cope with the demands of a mass Labour Movement and revolutionary class conflict would then result. Welfare reform is thus seen as an important part of the *strategic objective* of creating a revolutionary socialist movement.[26] (Incidentally it may well be plausible to analyse the desired Communist society in terms of welfare—but it should not be forgotten that the establishment of such a society requires, as a necessary though not sufficient condition, the abolition of class rule. There is no evidence that this can be achieved without revolutionary action.)

On your second point, from a Marxist viewpoint, the present role of State institutions is by definition supportive of the *status quo*—and this must include social work. If any radical change is to come about then these institutions must make a conscious effort to change direction. The fundamental structure of society is still based upon the private ownership of property: the increasing importance of the

State has led to a partnership between public and private sectors—but a partnership where the interests and assumptions of the *private* sector have remained dominant. Consequently the State in the economic and industrial sphere has been subordinate to, and virtually an adjunct of, the capitalist system. Far from supplanting the capitalist system, the State has become absorbed into a new form of capitalist structure.

Equally important though, Marxists, or most of them, would dispute your assertion that the Labour Movement in its present organizational and ideological form, represents the vehicle for achieving socialist change. As was argued earlier both the Trade Unions and the Labour Party are seen as having been absorbed to a very large extent into the existing political structure. Far from fulfilling an even potentially socialist role the Labour Party has ceased to be even a reformist party in any meaningful sense.[27] 'Civic freedoms' are indeed an important part of our political culture and are largely the achievement of the Labour Movement. But as society is further bureaucratized and the Labour Party itself becomes the agency of bureaucratic control, it is again necessary to think in terms of a real socialist alternative to the existing structure, precisely in order to protect these very freedoms.

C.P. From the democratic socialist viewpoint this grossly underestimates the potential for change within the Labour Movement and overestimates the ease with which a new party could be created. One of the key features of British political culture has been the *stability* of the superstructure even when under great strain because of rapid socio-economic changes.

The stability so characteristic of British political culture has provided the ideal framework for the growth of moderate, integrated and *successful* evolutionary movements; and has also resulted in repeated examples of potentially revolutionary movements being transformed into more moderate, progressive organizations which have built up foundations upon which further reforms have been able to take place. There has been a persistent resistance to revolution in this country virtually from the time of the French Revolution (by the vast majority of the population). To try to create a new force on the Left, ignoring the continuities inherent in the British system, really is 'pie in the sky'.

R.T. But the Labour Party was created in the space of a few years—and contrary to expectations (and even the intentions of its early leaders) it quickly emerged as a major political force. The evidence that it is no longer fulfilling a socialist role (assuming that it ever did), and is incapable of ever doing so, now seems so overwhelming, that the task of creating a new force is essential.[28]

This must be the central task for Marxists. The major obstacle lies neither in the weakness of the Labour leaders, nor in the progress of capitalism to a more humane and liberal structure but rather, first, in the ability of the capitalist establishment, especially in Britain, to give way when and where necessary, in advance of major conflict, whilst always retaining the essentials of power and privilege; and second, in the widespread, sophisticated and often unconscious use of the whole range of mediating institutions which legitimate capitalist ideology. Hence the crucial importance to Marxism of the legitimation debate (see Chapter 6).

Capitalism relies very heavily on the power of ideas to maintain the existing system: no longer is physical coercion the major means of ensuring compliance—increasingly people are being consistently socialized through powerful State agencies into an acceptance of the fundamental values of capitalism. Yet at the same time free communication is an established right and there is a real opportunity for socialist ideas to be propagated (through socialist newspapers, etc.) and create a positive ideological alternative to the mounting chaos of capitalism. The fact that the Labour Movement is more concerned to salvage the existing structure (e.g. Incomes Policy) than implant socialist consciousness, again demonstrates the lack of commitment of the Labour Movement to socialist change.

C.P. The opportunity for propagating socialist ideas does exist— and I agree that it must be taken—but what the democratic socialist argues is that this change must be both evolutionary and democratic (in the sense of representing majority opinion), if society is to avoid minority totalitarian rule. Existing institutions do, of course, need radicalizing but the social cost of major restructuring over a short period is very high. And, as Bevan reflected, the 'average man' would not welcome a redistribution of wealth—especially if this were to be a more equitable distribution between the rich Western countries and the Third World whose poverty still acts as a main support of the relatively exalted life style we *all* enjoy in the West.[29] Can you realistically expect that the 'apolitical mass' would accept such a sudden and drastic cut in living standards?

R.T. I am not advocating 'sudden and drastic change'. But I am convinced that we need to build up, ideologically and organizationally, an *alternative* to the existing capitalist structure. Moreover, to imply that socialism would mean great hardship and misery for everyone for a long time is quite erroneous: part of the justification for a socialist system is precisely that it will be *more* efficient, *more* rational and *more* just (economically as well as socially).

Reform, revolution, or . . . ?

We are obviously reaching an impasse but before we leave our general argument I would add one final point about totalitarianism. Certainly Marxists disregard the dangers of an 'absolutist' communist rule at their peril: but one of the major themes of the 'New Left' has been the total rejection of the Stalinist, centralist orthodoxy and the re-affirmation of the humanist aspirations of the 'true' Marxist tradition.[30] The tradition of freedom within the British political culture is a vital part of the transformation to a socialist system and any movement which failed to preserve *and extend* these freedoms would be invalid. Indeed one of the tremendous advantages that Britain has, in the last decades of the twentieth century, compared say with Russia in 1917, is the very existence of this mature and sophisticated political culture, which in itself acts as a bulwark against the dangers of totalitarianism. The bogey of Stalinist-style dictatorship has been too often used to discredit revolutionary ideas in Western Europe.

C.P. Unfortunately, it is not only Stalinist autocracy that is at issue. By its very nature a revolutionary movement throws up a leadership, and it would be naïve to expect any such leadership to surrender power voluntarily or to allow a wide degree of freedom to opponents. The grisly example of Allende's Chile will serve as a warning to any revolutionary who cherishes ideas of immediate and near-total freedom for an 'opposition' in a revolutionary situation. (Even in the Western 'democracies' it is very exceptional for politicians to surrender power voluntarily—the only two examples amongst twentieth-century British Prime Ministers—Baldwin and Wilson—do not inspire confidence; both may have feared what was to come, or hoped for a future recall to resolve the 'national crisis'.)

The danger of a Marxist totalitarian regime may be real—and social workers who blithely call for revolution should consider these implications—yet a *far* more dangerous threat comes from the 'Right'. On the 'Hard Right' the National Front has been enlarging its support steadily over the last few years. An extrapolation of the General Election results since 1959 shows that those voting for Communist Party candidates (or other declared Marxists) outside the Labour Party, were outnumbered 2:1 by those voting National Front. While the highest ever recorded vote for the Communist Party was 103,000 in 1945, the Extreme Right vote rose from 12,000 in 1954 to 115,000 between 1970 and 1974.[31] Before discarding hard-won parliamentary democratic freedom in favour of the Pandora's box of revolution, Marxists should weigh very carefully the likely result of a Left versus Right conflict.

R.T. The implication of your argument is that 'human nature' will corrupt any revolutionary leadership, however genuine its original intentions. This seems to me a false assumption; 'human nature' is not static or given, it is to a very large extent moulded by the total environment. One of the underlying arguments for a revolutionary movement is precisely that it needs a strong, determined and mutually reinforcing socialist sub-culture to formulate and maintain a genuinely socialist perspective. Power does indeed corrupt, but if the socialist commitment is strong enough and if the democratic traditions are deeply rooted enough, then there is far less likelihood of totalitarian oppression developing. Such dangers are only partly psychological in origin: given the appropriate socialist commitment to freedom, and positive, democratic political culture, there is every reason for the socialist revolution to be both 'democratic' and 'socialist'!

On your second point, there can be no doubt of the threat from the Right (although I would take the possibility of a Right swing within official Conservatism as more worrying than the growth of the crude, racist Fascism of the National Front: at present all the major parties reject this obscene ideology, although I agree that it is by no means inconceivable that the Conservatives will incorporate an overtly racist stance as part of their present 'lurch to the Right'). But Marxists hold that the deepening crisis of capitalism is inevitable: it may well be that this crisis will be resolved, in the short-term, by the victory of some form of right-wing corporatism, but it is the task of the Labour Movement to counter this and ensure that it is socialism that ultimately arises from the chaos of capitalism. You really do seem to imply that if we all sit tight and continue to believe in the social democratic and liberal values, nasty things like Fascism will disappear—this seems both historically and ideologically naïve, and not a little dangerous!

C.P. We obviously disagree about the means of achieving the socialist system we are both aiming for. Let us look at how these different perspectives view the specific roles of social work. There is agreement that social work has the potential to perform an invaluable political function. For the democratic socialist, social work is a part of a complex of State agencies that must act as catalysts for social change—a key institution in the evolutionary movement, persuading government, individuals and organizations of the need for 'practical' humanitarian change *and* a long-term restructuring of society. Moreover, social work has this unique bi-directional position in society, mediating between 'clients' and society and vice versa. It must therefore develop a clearly defined self-image and a conscious socio-political role, for it has an important part to play in the creation of an effective democratic society. A central objective of the social worker's task is to enable people to maintain their individuality and fulfil their civic and social functions,[32] aiming to aid in furthering the client's autonomy and self-actualization. Through this enabling role the social worker is not only aiding in the relief of human misery but creating also the essential conditions for the operation of a democratic system.

R.T. Nobody would dispute the 'self-actualizing' role of social work—what is at issue is the best means of fulfilling this task. The Marxist argues that whilst there is an absolute need for humanitarian individual care, any sustained long-term improvement in individual welfare depends, in the vast majority of cases, upon changes in the social environment: in a shift from a capitalist to a socialist system, where public and community needs would be the criteria for action and socialist values would be the norm, not the exception. Not only does this apply in direct material ways—for example in the maldistribution of resources where office blocks rather than houses are built—but also in general social terms: the alienation of the worker, particularly in the production line system, as a result of the wage labour structure existing under capitalism, the neuroses created by the insistence upon such things as material wealth, competition, status and so on. The objective is certainly to enable people to 'actualize their potential'—but this is simply impossible under capitalism. Consequently, the major thrust of social work, as with the other 'service and welfare' professions, must be towards the creation of a socialist system.

C.P. Again, we are not in disagreement over long-term objectives but rather over method—the development of a practical humanitarian care, informed by what is best in the professional concept, can further the democratization and restructuring of the system along socialist lines.

There is, however, a glaring omission in your prognosis: there is only about 20 per cent of the population in modern Britain living at or near the subsistence level; obviously this is a disgracefully high figure, but in terms of historical development, it demonstrates great progress. At the same time the majority of the population are living relatively comfortably, entrenched in a highly materialistic life-style: unlike Lenin's workers, they have considerably more to lose than their chains: as mentioned earlier, both Bevan and Shaw recognized, sadly, that should the 'working man's' material needs be satisfied, he would be unlikely to show much interest in politics. To attempt drastic change in these circumstances would surely lead to totalitarian repression—Left or Right. Democratic socialists must strive instead for the creation of an alternative socialist consciousness. Perhaps the most damning single criticism of the Labour Party is its almost complete inability, and apparent unwillingness, to propagate socialist ideas. Through their unwillingness to stress the positive alternative which socialism offers—and their pandering to the lowest common denominator demands of the ballot box, the Labour Party has, since 1945, virtually ignored the core differences between socialist and capitalist goals.

In the social work context this means, first, giving weight to individual, humanitarian care (which, despite your assertions, Marxists often seem to be in danger of overlooking), and second, creating a force for socialist ideas through the professional organization to convince people and groups of the need for socialist planning within the whole of the welfare social service field.

At the pressure-group level, of course, social work must be seen to be a responsible, informed and 'integrated' profession which can argue a strong and authoritative case in favour of greater resources. Any major commitment to overtly subversive objectives would mean a drastic repudiation of social work by both the political machine and the electorate. We must recognize that until the general public are better informed and able to assess the implications of real socialist alternatives, social work must avoid seeming to be too far ahead or it may appear unintelligible to the community and thus fall an easy prey to reactionary forces. Social work has a role to play in the development of socialist consciousness: the moral impetus is there, both in the profession and in the wider Labour Movement. Bevan pointed the direction:[33]

> What is national planning but an insistence that human beings shall make ethical choices on a national scale—the language of priorities is the religion of socialism, economic planning to serve *a moral purpose* [my italics].

Maybe it will be thought that I am being over-optimistic? But comparing Bevan's opponents of the 1940s and 1950s, who considered planning an anathema, with today's mainstream supporters of capitalism who now completely accept the notion of a planned, mixed economy, it seems that we have come some way along the road towards socialism. For, after all, Marx, almost a hundred years ago, recognized that the extension of the parliamentary franchise would force changes in favour of the general population.[34] Perhaps the greatest problem is that sometimes the gains made are less distributive than they appear, often being paid for by the 'working class';[35] nevertheless, the potential for further democratic evolution undoubtedly exists.

R.T. Let's take these arguments one at a time. First, it is a complete misunderstanding of Marxism to imagine that because workers become better off materially they automatically become more middle class. Numerous empirical surveys have, anyway, disproved this 'embourgoisement' thesis.[36] Indeed it is not the workers at 'the bottom of the pile' who are the most militant: compare the shopworkers to the miners for example! Class consciousness depends upon a whole range of complex factors over and above living standards. (Incidentally, Lenin realized that one of his major problems in creating a revolutionary movement lay precisely in the absence of any sizable, effective and firmly-based proletariat in Russia in 1917!)

Even more important, in our present context, is the deepening crisis of capitalism. Between 1945 and 1970 we experienced a prolonged period of stability and expansion, but the fundamental imbalance of capitalism has now reasserted itself and the much vaunted affluence of Western society is looking distinctly less secure as unemployment and inflation soar upwards. The essential task for all socialists in this situation is to link the economic struggle to the political movement for socialism. This leads in to your second point: of course, the task for socialism is to create an 'alternative socialist consciousness'—this is what I have just argued—but this must be linked into a strategy for action, and to be *effective* this action must take place *outside* the existing structures and have a clear socialist perspective.

To try to convince people that the existing organizations of the Labour Movement can be changed into vehicles for socialist change is totally mistaken—and will lead to frustration, disillusionment and thus a serious weakening of the potential for real socialist change. Third, social work must act as a pressure group—but surely not from within an 'integrated' (i.e. capitalist-oriented) position but from a stance based upon ideological strength which differentiates itself and its objectives from the ethos of capitalism.

Finally, the changes since 1945 have indeed been dramatic, but I would argue that the increasing involvement of the State in capitalist industry represents not an advance towards socialism, but a further and very significant drift into the monopoly capitalism that Marx predicted. 'Planning' has not been used as a means of socialist change in any sense. The vague platitudes of Bevan never meant much and certainly were not translated into action (always excepting the NHS). Nationalization resulted in the freeing of private capital (through compensation) for more profitable reinvestment elsewhere.[37] In the long run, this saw 'public industry' subsidizing private capitalism. Also, the much vaunted 'planning' far from leading to a decentralization of control and a redistribution of power (and income) has accelerated the trend to bureaucratic, central

Reform, revolution, or . . . ?

control. Capitalism will not be 'reformed' by such social democratic innovations, it will merely be assisted in its ability to adapt and absorb.

C.P. I must confess to some amazement that a Marxist should complain about the risks to democracy of bureaucratic control in the admittedly piecemeal planning achievements of the first post-War Labour government. It seems that you would have your planning cake and eat it. Marxism, or rather Leninism, gave to the world the horrors of central party control and discipline, the 'dictatorship of the proletariat'. Hardly a democratic structure!

To be fair, the problem of bureaucracy—the choking effects of a huge administrative apparatus—seems to be experienced by all modern societies, irrespective of ideology. The complex problems of implementing change need not only a bureaucratic structure but, above all, *time* to adjust both institutions and social attitudes to a new situation. Hence the inherent fallacy in Marxism of being able to 'free people' by revolutionizing society: the TIME required to bring about real change in the environment and therefore man himself, is more than one lifetime; only an evolutionary scale is tenable, otherwise short-term gains will, at best, be lost by 'fatigue' of the socialist commitment and enthusiasm—or, at worst, be imposed by repression, which itself would require a 'new' revolution to restore the balance of freedoms.

Generally, these Marxist ideas seem rather naïve, and certainly dangerous. To jettison the historical relationship with the Labour Movement, to try to act as a pressure group outside the institutional structure is simplistic in the extreme and in the case of social work would likely result in the emasculation of the profession, leaving an over-compliant 'rump' which would be of little long-term service to clients. The only *viable* perspective entails working within the existing structure and pressing for more radical change. If it were to do otherwise, social work would be in real danger of risking the supreme arrogance, where the professional sets himself above his client, and splits himself off from his client's perception and understanding. Dishonest means produce corrupted ends—however 'genuine' the intention.

Our system is very far from perfect—but to try to change it through the revolutionary process you suggest would entail massive human suffering and run the risk of precipitating a holocaust. Have Marxists *really* thought through the *meaning* of revolution . . .?

Another essential part of the democratic concept which Marxists consistently ignore or underrate is the need for free expression of differences—of opinion, taste, culture and so on. Marxists tend to assume uniformity and do not give sufficient weight to the need for variety and for conflict—within the limits of social order. Unless socialists realize these inherent needs, the result of socialism is again likely to be a totalitarian system.

R.T. Perhaps we are not so far apart as this interchange implies. The Marxist does not argue for sudden change brought about through a 'power putsch' by a minority; on the contrary the whole burden of Marx's analysis lay in the dual progress of class consciousness through objective economic factors, and the role of the revolutionary party in stimulating socialist organization and ideas. Through this process there would be created a genuine mass movement of the working class and its allies, whose clear historic role would be to bring about the socialist society. Marxists are therefore concerned to stimulate socialist activity leading to the formation of a viable mass socialist movement: the only true democracy resides within the process of mass activity to create a socialist system, reinforced by the civic freedoms already intrinsic to the political culture of the British Labour Movement.

Marxists do not suggest 'jettisoning the historical relationship with the Labour Movement' but building upon that experience to create *new* institutions and *new* vehicles for socialist change.[38] In this perspective social work has a potentially crucial role to play—particularly in the community work field where situations involving direct political action and affiliations occur all the time. Do community workers, for example, encourage tenants' groups to work closely with Labour Councils avoiding 'conflict' with authority where possible? It depends of course on specific circumstances, but surely, in the majority of cases, the building of an alternative organization allied to, at the very least, a healthy scepticism of the Labour Party's role is a more *realistic* perspective, and one less likely to lead to dashed hopes and frustration?

On your last point, I do agree that to an extent Marxists have underestimated the need for diversity within a social system, although again this weakness is one with which the 'New Left' has been consistently concerned. However, I must make explicit one fundamental point: Marxists hold that the *structural reason for conflict lies within the class system*: different social classes have differing and conflicting needs and no amount of 'rational discussion' can alter this. If we assume a classless, socialist society then the basic social reasons for conflict will have been removed. I would want to draw a sharp distinction between the positive desirability of diversity and choice within the framework of socialist democracy, and the need to eradicate structural, and therefore inevitable, conflict which can be accomplished only within a socialist system.

(Incidentally, your identification of Marxism with bureaucracy is indicative of the tragic legacy of Stalinism. The whole purpose of the socialization of industry within both the Marxist tradition *and* the Left social-democrat movement, has not been to create public corporations and therefore centralized, bureaucratic control: the emphasis has on the contrary been upon the opportunities for decentralization, for workers' control and ultimately for an end to industrial alienation, which public ownership can, potentially, offer!)

C.P. In the long-term it *may* be necessary, and possible, to create a new alignment on the Left. At the moment this is not possible and we must work with what we have. For social workers, this means working from the existing institutional position.

To sum up, there seem to me to be major weaknesses in the Marxists' analysis (not least in their failure to appreciate the crucial time factor); but far greater dangers arising from the historical experience of trying to put Marxism into practice: in every case a catalogue of human suffering, suppression of freedom and stifling bureaucratization. This experience strengthens my belief that to achieve the socialist system we both envisage, progress must be both evolutionary and democratic: in the British context this must mean working through the existing mass organizations of the Labour Movement: the Labour Party and the Trade Unions.

In the context of social work, this means a politicized and radical social work profession—but one which is clearly and unambiguously operating within the central structure of society, and attempting to exert influence from within. At the same time social work must never sacrifice its primary concern with the welfare of the individual to wider ideological concerns.

A criticism sometimes made of the democratic-socialist social worker is that we are too anxious about the present, and consequently afraid of 'strife' and that the evolutionary orientation implies an acceptance of the 'consensus' model of society, ignoring the 'conflict' reality.[39] Earlier (Chapter 5) we looked at the role of social work in relation to concepts of 'comfort, change, control and conflict'. We suggested that there were considerable overlaps which resulted from the partially shared aetiological value-systems.

In my view a similar situation applies to ideological analyses of the structure of society—I see the models of 'consensus, control, conflict' as a continuum of the dynamics of power; at any given moment a society may be shifting within this dynamic equilibrium and thus some sort of balance of power is achieved—not necessarily because of genuine agreement, but via a number of strategies which produces accommodation between the antagonistic forces.

The 'consensus' view of society need not therefore be taken to imply a static, harmonious structure—but rather be seen as a continuous process of evolutionary change where any inherent conflicts may be resolved. Thus a consensus model does not exclude or deny conflict structures within society: on the contrary, 'consensus' implicitly recognizes that there are differing 'parties' to be brought together.

Control may also be perceived within this power-dynamic and might be construed as an imbalance of consensus, or the result of overwhelming conflict which can only be temporarily resolved by repression. Nevertheless, where control features are dominant in a society, oppositional forces will ultimately re-emerge with new conflict generating the impetus for change: either further crushing domination or a new consensus.

In the context of modern society, where total destruction is literally possible, it may be that the conflicting forces within our society finally recognize the need for institutional mechanisms to reduce the conflict element, even though it means change and, cumulatively, radical change. Social work is one such 'institution' which serves legitimately the dual purpose of reaching a consensus through conflict, and creating a changing social order without precipitating societal dislocations and breakdown.

R.T. To reply very briefly: for the reasons I have given it seems to me that Marxist analysis provides the framework for analysing contemporary society—although of course an enormous amount remains to be done. The undoubted faults of twentieth-century communist societies must not and cannot be brushed aside—but these are attributable, in my view, to eradicable organizational and ideological flaws within socialist parties and thinking, and cannot be traced back to metaphysical theories of 'human nature'. It is the task of modern socialist movements to devise ways and means of avoiding these tragic mistakes in the future. In the British context it has, in my view, been shown beyond all shadow of doubt that the Labour Party is not, and can never be, a socialist party. To divert energies into an attempt to radicalize the organization is guaranteed to fail. If socialism is to come to Britain, new vehicles building upon the experience and mistakes of the old, must be created.

I fail to see how any socialist who accepts class analysis can argue in favour of a consensus model of society—either as a description or a prescription. As socialists we would surely both accept that consensus arguments put forward by apologists for capitalism are merely ideological camouflage for what is a fundamentally exploitative, class-structured system? There can be no consensus between conflicting social classes: this is not a question of 'will' or 'tolerance' or 'pulling together in the national interest'—different social classes have sharply differing objective economic and political interests, and only through struggle will these be resolved. To achieve this transition from capitalism to socialism the creation of a 'socialist consciousness' is essential.

Social work has, or could have, an important role to play in building this alternative 'socialist consciousness' which is an absolute prerequisite for the creation of any serious mass socialist movement. This is not to deny the importance of individual social work care, rather to put it in the correct ideological context.

C.P. This seems to outline our different orientations reasonably clearly. There are, though, several areas of agreement which we might also mention. One concerted theme running throughout the book is that social work is inevitably 'political' and that the profession needs to come to terms with its dual responsibility as both a 'welfare' and a 'political' institution to create a properly cohesive and coherent structure. From our socialist perspectives we would also agree that a social work commitment to the creation of a socialist system is a vital part, not only of the social work role, but of the wider movement towards a restructuring of the social system.

In the context of the British attempt to create a socialist society, we would also agree wholeheartedly with Rosa Luxemburg's condemnation of the Bolsheviks' use of coercion: 'draconian penalties, rule by terror, all these things are but palliatives. The only way to rebirth is the school of public life itself—*the most unlimited, the broadest democracy* and public opinion. It is rule by fear which demoralises'[40] (my italics). This is the 'democratic component' which is so essential for the achievement of any viable socialist system.

R.T. Yes, I agree.[41] But, in addition, we must not forget that whatever form(s) it takes, conflict and struggle will be necessary to achieve a socialist society. The role of the socialist remains as Marx and Engels characterized it in 1848:[42]

> But they [the Communists] never cease, for a single instant, to instil into the working class the clearest possible recognition of the hostile antagonism between bourgeoisie and proletariat . . . .

Social work, as a potentially radical institution in modern society, has an important part to play in this process.

References

Chapter one: Social work and politics: an introduction

1 B. Crick, *In Defence of Politics,* Penguin Books, 1962, p. 21.
2 R. Lees, *Politics and Social Work,* Routledge & Kegan Paul, 1972, p. xi.
3 Reflected in Sir Keith Joseph's concept of the 'cycle of deprivation' which is severely criticized by W. Jordan, *Poor Parents: Social Policy and the Cycle of Deprivation,* Routledge & Kegan Paul, 1974.
4 E.g. M. E. Richmond's classic definition of social casework as 'cooperating with them to achieve at one and the same time *their own and society's betterment*' (our italics), M. Richmond, *Social Diagnosis,* Russell Sage Foundation, 1917.
5 See K. Woodroofe, *From Charity to Social Work,* Routledge & Kegan Paul, 1962, where it is suggested that the 'psychiatric deluge' influenced social work education and aspirations profoundly in the 1940s and 1950s.
6 See R. Bitensky who links the changing theoretical ethos of social casework with macro socio-economic developments in the USA, R. Bitensky, 'Influence of Political Power in Determining the Theoretical Development of Social Work', *Journal of Social Policy,* 2. 2. 1975, pp. 119-29.
7 Although Barbara Castle had no doubts: 'Get into the political fight', she urged BASW in 1972. Quoted in G. Mungham, 'Social Workers and Political Action', in H. Jones (ed.), *Towards a New Social Work,* Routledge & Kegan Paul, 1975. More recently representatives of the three major political parties have welcomed the opportunity to speak directly to BASW members. E.g., D. Ennals, 'Six Contentious Months as Secretary of State', *Social Work Today,* 8.1.1976 and 'Hopes for 1977', *Social Work Today,* 8.9.1976.
8 E.g., Z. Butrym, *The Nature of Social Work,* Macmillan, 1976.
9 This is clearly reflected in the CCETSW document, Paper No. 13, *Values in Social Work,* 1976, where the role of social work in relation to societal, philosophical and political values is discussed. It is pointed out that social workers must 'consider the place of social

work within the structure of capitalist society of which they are a part', para. 4, 22.
10 BASW, through the pages of *Social Work Today,* frequently asserts pressure-group role in relation to Ministers and Members of Parliament—e.g., 'BASW to Make TV Programme', *Social Work Today,* February 1977. Also the frequency with which politicians, in and out of government, write in the BASW journal suggests that they possibly see BASW in a political role; see, for example, *Letters:* E. Deakins, Under-Secretary of State, DHSS, 21.12.76; J. Lloyd, Chairman Housing Committee, Stockport, 8.2.77; D. Ennals, *op. cit.*
11 R. Miliband, *Parliamentary Socialism,* 2nd edn, Merlin Press, 1973, p. 376.
12 Some explanation of the terms 'democratic socialism' and 'social democracy', both of which are used in the text, is perhaps necessary. We use the term 'social democracy' to refer, broadly, to the central, mainstream, 'Labourist' belief system of the British Labour Party. 'Democratic socialism', on the other hand, is used to refer to that persistent and continuous trend within the Labour Party which stresses the necessity for radical but gradualist socialist change within a democratic and parliamentary framework. This general ideological trend finds expression in the 'orthodox' Labour Left—from the early ILP, through the Bevanites, to the contemporary 'Tribune' group.
13 This is illustrated by Priscilla Young in the Foreword to CCETSW Paper No. 13: 'Values are central to commitment and to *action in social work* . . .', who thus accepts that the ideological position held by social workers will determine their professional action.
14 See the enormous increase in 'social work legislation': since 1969, the Children and Young Persons Act (1969), the Local Authority Social Services Act (1970), the National Health Service Act (1974), the Children Act (1975). Also, many Acts have been passed which increase the scope of social work activity—for example, as 'child advocate' under the Children Act (1975)—and social workers are increasingly expected to 'control deviants'.

Chapter two: Tolerating uncertainty

1 A. Marwick, *War and Social Change in the Twentieth Century,* Macmillan, 1974.
2 R. Dahrendorf, *The New Liberty,* Routledge & Kegan Paul, 1975.
3 A. Solzhenitzyn, *Warning to the Western World,* Bodley Head and BBC Publications, 1976.
4 Noel Timms, *Social Casework,* Routledge & Kegan Paul, 1964.
5 See, for example, R. Bailey and M. Brake (eds), *Radical Social Work,* Arnold, 1975; H. Jones (ed.), *Towards a New Social Work,* Routledge & Kegan Paul, 1975; W. Jordan, *Freedom and the Welfare State,* Routledge & Kegan Paul, 1976.
6 G. B. Shaw, *Complete Plays—The Apple Cart,* Odhams Press, 1934.
7 K. Woodroofe, *From Charity to Social Work,* Routledge & Kegan Paul, 1962.

8 B. Smith, *Policy Making in British Government*, Martin Robertson, 1976, p. 187.
9 See J. Algie, *Social Values, Objectives and Action*, Kogan Page, 1974.
10 In the CCETSW Paper No. 10, *Education and Training for Social Work*, CCETSW has listed some of the academic disciplines contributing to social work: amongst these are sociology, political science, economics and the study of social policy and administration.
11 G. Fowler, 'The Politics of Social Administration', unpublished paper at Annual General Meeting, Social Administration Committee of the JUC, 1977.
12 H. M. Bartlett, *Common Base of Social Work Practice*, National Association of Social Workers, New York, 1970. The emphasis is upon 'generalism', but also on the question of purpose, as she seeks to conceive of social work in a unified way. This approach has been given impetus by H. Goldstein, *Social Work Practice—A Unitary Approach*, Columbia University Press, 1973, addressing itself to the totality of the task facing the social worker—significantly combining those extra client factors, such as community and resources, with the more traditional concern of interpersonal relationships.
13 Besides Goldstein, *op. cit.*, see A. Pincus and A. Minahan, *Social Work Practice, Model and Method*, Peacock, 1973.
14 R. Baker, *Interpersonal Process in Generic Social Work*, Preston Institute of Technology Press, Victoria, Australia, 1976.
15 R. Evans, 'Some Implications of an Integrated Model of Social Work for Theory and Practice', *British Journal of Social Work*, 6.2. 1976, pp. 177-200.
16 Z. Butrym, *The Nature of Social Work*, Macmillan, 1976.
17 W. Jordan, *op. cit.*
18 R. Holman, *Poverty*, Martin Robertson, 1977.
19 G. Pearson, *The Deviant Imagination*, Macmillan, 1975.
20 P. Leonard, 'Towards a Paradigm for Radical Practice', pp. 46-62 in R. Bailey and M. Brake, *op. cit.*
21 P. Townsend (ed.), *The Concept of Poverty*, Heinemann, 1970. See also A. B. Atkinson's *Economics of Inequality*, Oxford University Press, 1975, for a more recent analysis of some of the structural factors associated with poverty; also R. Holman, *op. cit.*
22 See, for examples of American 'schools' of social work, R. Roberts and R. Nee, *Theories of Social Casework*, University of Chicago Press, 1970. Also R. Evans, *op. cit.*
23 See, for example, G. Pearson, 'The Politics of Uncertainty', in H. Jones (ed.), *Towards a New Social Work*, Routledge & Kegan Paul, 1975, pp. 45-68; and *The Radical Therapists*, Penguin Books, 1974.
24 K. Woodroofe, *op. cit.*
25 Z. Butrym, *op. cit.*
26 D. Gath, B. Cooper, F. Gattoni and D. Rockett, *Child Guidance and Delinquency in a London Borough*, Oxford University Press, 1977.
27 Noel Timms, 'Child Guidance Service—A Pilot Study', in G. MacLachlan (ed.), *Problems and Progress in Medical Care*, Routledge & Kegan Paul, 1968.
28 CCETSW Paper No. 13, *Values in Social Work*, 1976.

29 R. Plant, *Social and Moral Theory in Casework*, Routledge & Kegan Paul, 1970.
30 W. J. Patterson, *Social Work's Theory of Man*—Occasional Papers, New University, Ulster, 1976. See also H. A. Prins, 'Motivation for Social Work', *Social Work Today*, 5.2.1974, for an analysis of the contribution of religious orientation to social work.
31 W. Jordan, *op. cit.*, for a fuller discussion on this point.
32 This theme, it could be argued, runs throughout the CCETSW Paper No. 13, *op. cit.*
33 For a Marxist analysis of this problem, see R. Miliband, *The State in Capitalist Society*, Weidenfeld & Nicolson, 1969.
34 By community workers not least, see D. Jones and M. Mayo, *Community Work: Two*, Routledge & Kegan Paul, 1975.
35 W. Jordan, *op. cit.*, p. 79.
36 *A Code of Ethics for Social Workers*, BASW, 1975.
37 F. Biesteck, *The Casework Relationship*, Allen & Unwin, 1961.
38 P. Seed, *The Expansion of Social Work in Britain*, Routledge & Kegan Paul, 1973.
39 Perhaps the classical dichotomy is seen in the task of the Probation Officer who 'befriends' yet is an officer of the court which punishes and prohibits.
40 CCETSW, Paper No. 13, *op. cit.*
41 G. B. Shaw, *op. cit.*
42 CCETSW, Paper No. 10, *op. cit.*
43 G. Fowler, *op. cit.*
44 E.g. J. K. Galbraith, *The Age of Uncertainty*, André Deutsch, 1977.

Chapter three: Political culture of contemporary Britain (1): Conservatism

1 R. Dowse and J. Hughes, *Political Sociology*, Wiley, 1972, Chapter 7,1, p. 227.
2 The *degree* of variance between ideologies in modern British (and Western) society is a matter of dispute between liberal pluralists and Marxists which raises fundamental issues of analysis (see Chapter 6).
3 We are using ideology here in the non-pejorative neutral sense of a system of thought. Raymond Williams has usefully categorized the various uses of the terms in his *Keywords*, Fontana, 1976: the 'Napoleonic pejorative': an abstract, false revolutionary system of ideas; the 'Marxist pejorative': idealist constructs to explain, through a false consciousness, an alien environment; and the 'Marxist neutral': a system of ideas appropriate to a given class (see pp. 127-9).
4 The late Anthony Crosland, formerly leading social democratic theorist of the present Labour Party (*The Conservative Enemy, The Future of Socialism*, etc.), and George Brown, the anti-intellectual, working-class trade unionist, par excellence.
5 For fuller information on the various aspects of the subject see Bibliography.
6 Nigel Harris, *Competition and the Corporate Society*, Methuen, 1972, p. 11.

7 Q. Hogg, *The Case for Conservatism*, Penguin Books, 1947, p. 13. Less colourfully, but none the less vehemently, Lord Butler (in his autobiography, *The Art of the Possible,* Hamish Hamilton, 1971, p. 28) emphasizes a similar view of Conservative politics as embodying a continuing and vibrant tradition:

> What they [the 'captains of Toryism'] had left us . . . was not a collection of causes for which we were obliged to die in the last ditch, nor a set of premises by whose consistent application we might infallibly regularize our conduct, but a mature tradition of political thought and behaviour which is neither fixed nor finished. This tradition at its best is responsive to the demands of each new age, empirical as to method, resourceful in expressing itself in popular idiom, though deeply conscious that 'The councils to which Time is not called, Time will not ratify'.

8 E.g., M. Oakeshott, 'On Being a Conservative' in *Rationalism in Politics*, Methuen, 1962.
9 Sir Geoffrey Butler, *The Tory Tradition,* Conservative Political Centre, 1957, quoted in S. H. Beer, *Modern British Politics*, Faber & Faber, 2nd edn, 1969, p. 93.
10 E.g., D. Fraser, *The Evolution of the British Welfare State,* Macmillan, 1973.
11 S. H. Beer, *op. cit.*
12 *Ibid.*, p. 3.
13 E.g., Erich Fromm, *Fear of Freedom,* Routledge & Kegan Paul, 1969.
14 D. Offer and J. L. Offer, 'Growing-up: a follow-up study of normal adolescents', *Seminar Psychiatry,* 1.1.1969, pp. 46-56.
15 For the main works by Burke, see Bibliography.
16 Whilst this belief may not have been given explicit recognition until the late nineteenth century, the assumptions dependent upon the rationality argument underlie much of earlier Conservative thinking.
17 Of particular importance in relation to social democracy is the key place that this argument holds in the development of Fabian thinking.
18 I.e., the laws giving protection via tariffs to home-grown corn against competition from imported corn.
19 The third alternative, the romantic alliance suggested by the Young England group between 'the aristocracy' and 'the poor' against 'industrialism', never really got off the ground: as R. Blake, *The Conservative Party from Peel to Churchill*, Fontana, 1972, pp. 23-5, points out, not only did their ideas conflict with the 'spirit of the age', the dominant capitalist ethos—in practical terms their strategy was doomed because the class to which they wished to appeal did not have the vote, and therefore had no political power.
20 R. Blake, *op. cit.* This gives an excellent, clear and concise account (from a viewpoint very sympathetic to the Conservative Party) of the historical and political questions involved in this transition.
21 N. Harris, *op. cit.*, p. 23:

> The creation of (modern) Conservatism was the result of two related processes: the absorption of Liberal ideas by the aristocratic leaders of the party, and the movement towards a more limited version of

Liberalism by increasing numbers of businessmen. The marriage created Liberal-Conservatism.
22 For a concise account of this process, see N. Harris, *op. cit.*, part 1.
23 *Ibid.*, pp. 285-6.
24 Crystal Palace speech, Tory Democrat, quoted in N. Harris, *op. cit.*, p. 287.
25 E.g., Nine Hours Act; T.U. legislation; Public Health Act, etc.
26 E.g. Cecil Rhodes quoted in *Imperialism: The Highest Stage of Capitalism* by V. I. Lenin, 1916 (1939, New York edn): 'The Empire . . . is a bread and butter question. If you want to avoid Civil War, you must become imperialists.'
27 See, for example, G. W. Allport, *The Nature of Prejudice*, Addison-Wesley, 1954.
28 N. Harris, *op. cit.*, p. 288.
29 R. Blake, *op. cit.*, p. 272.
30 Recent research has shown the surprising extent of the integration of the new industrial and commercial élites with the old landed aristocratic families.
31 Q. Hogg, *op. cit.*, pp. 66-70.
32 Title of R. A. Butler's autobiography, *op. cit.*
33 One excludes the extraordinary figure of Lord Home from the catalogue of post-War Conservative leaders: a throw-back to a past so far distant that it has almost disappeared.
34 Sir Keith Joseph and Sir Geoffrey Howe are the foremost economic theorists of the new 'radical Right'. Also, Sir Keith's election speeches in 1974 are an interesting example of the modern Conservative emphasis on the positive individualism of the Party's ideology.
35 N. Harris, *op. cit.*, *passim*.
36 *Ibid.*, p. 243.
37 *Ibid.*, *passim*.
38 Whether this should be a meritocratic or self-perpetuating governing class is an interesting theoretical ambivalence in modern Conservative thinking.
39 E.g., 'Toryism will yet arise from the tomb . . . to bring back strength to the Crown, liberty to the Subject, and to announce that power has only one duty—to secure the social welfare of the *PEOPLE.*' Benjamin Disraeli, *Sybil: or the Two Nations*, ch. 14, quoted in R. Blake, *op. cit.*, p. 5.
40 S. H. Beer, *op. cit.*, ch. 9, pp. 261-71.
41 See, for example, J. Kincaid, *Poverty and Equality in Britain*, Penguin Books, 1973; R. Blackburn, 'The Unequal Society', in J. Urry and J. Wakeford (eds), *Power in Britain*, Heinemann, 1973.
42 E.g., *Labour and the New Social Order*, 1918 policy document.
43 N. Harris, *op. cit.* This section draws heavily upon the final part of Harris's work: by far the most comprehensive Marxist analysis of modern Conservatism available.
44 *Ibid.*, p. 263.
45 *Ibid.*, pp. 263-4.
46 *Ibid.*, p. 254.

47 Often this is expressed in un-political forms in terms of a *working-class* distrust of 'the party of the bosses'. And almost always social democrats avoid use of Marxist terms of analysis when discussing the Conservative Party.
48 One has only to look at such modern examples of believing Conservatives as Lord Butler in *The Art of the Possible, op. cit.*; Quintin Hogg in *The Case for Conservatism, op. cit.*; and Lord Avon in his memoirs *The Eden Memoirs*, Cassell, 1960-5, to gain incontrovertible evidence of the sincerity of Conservative leaders.
49 E.g.: politically, the acceptance of a mixed economy, Keynesian fiscal policy, the Welfare State, and loss of Empire; socially, sexual permissiveness, at least lip-service to egalitarianism, and the continual battering of old-style Conservative values by the media.
50 Heath's record in this respect is impeccable and surely without equal (up to 1970!): a commitment to strong State involvement in an increasingly centralized industrial structure combined with a long-term vision of supra-national 'étatiste' policies in the EEC.

Chapter four: Political culture of contemporary Britain (2): social democracy

1 Raymond Williams, *Keywords*, Fontana, 1976, p. 150.
2 A comprehensive survey of British political culture and the place of social democracy within it has yet to be written. A number of useful articles is listed in the Bibliography—one of the more interesting being 'The origins of the present crisis', P. Anderson (ed.), in *Towards Socialism*, Fontana and New Left Books, 1965.
3 E.g., E. Burke's *Reflections on the Revolution in France* (first published 1790), Holst, New York, 1965.
4 From the later 1840s to the late 1870s the Trade Union movement was dominated by the 'New Model Trade Unions' of skilled artisans, dominated by liberal ideology, and construing Trade Union objectives in very 'pragmatic', 'moderate' terms (see pp. 45-8).
5 See J. Vincent, *The Formation of the British Liberal Party 1857-68*, Constable, 1966.
6 *Ibid.*, Introduction.
7 E.g., R. H. Tawney, *Religion and the Rise of Capitalism* (first published Murray, 1926), Penguin Books, 1964.
8 For a stimulating analysis of Nonconformism and its links with the developing consciousness of the English working class in the late eighteenth and early nineteenth centuries, see E. P. Thompson, *The Making of the English Working Class* (Gollancz, 1963), Penguin Books, 1968, ch. 11.
9 Hence, for example, the concern with temperance movements. For good accounts of the links between Liberalism and Nonconformity, see S. Koss, *Nonconformity in Modern British Politics*, Batsford, 1976, and D. Thompson, *Nonconformity in the Nineteenth Century*, Routledge & Kegan Paul, 1972.
10 See references, note 12.

11 There were, of course, major differences in policy over many issues—e.g. the Boer War—but the tempered radicalism of the party provided a common theoretical basis of agreement, even when the personalities involved were unable to see eye to eye.
12 For a full discussion of the reasons underlying the decline of the Liberal Party see J. A. Thompson, *The Collapse of the British Liberal Party*, Heath, 1961. Also G. Dangerfield, *The Strange Death of Liberal England*, MacGibbon & Kee, 1966; T. Wilson, *The Downfall of the Liberal Party 1914-35*, Fontana, 1968.
13 For recommended reading see Bibliography.
14 For what is still the best history and appreciation of Trade Unionism in general and the New Model Unions in particular, see S. and B. Webb, *History of Trade Unionism*, 2nd edn, Longmans, 1920.
15 See T. Nichols and P. Armstrong, *Workers Divided*, Fontana, 1976.
16 See Webbs, *op. cit.* (1920 edn), ch. 4.
17 See R. T. McKenzie, *British Political Parties*, Heinemann, rev. edn 1959, part 2, *passim*.
18 See K. W. Wedderburn, *The Worker and the Law*, Penguin Books, 1965, early chapters; H. Pelling, *History of Trade Unionism*, Macmillan, 1963; Webbs, *op. cit.*
19 This applies not only to the British working class but to the whole of British intellectual life. For a classic example of this obsessive anti-intellectualism (by an outstanding intellectual!) see Edward Thompson's open letter to Lesek Kolakowski, *Socialist Register*, Merlin Press, 1973 (ed. by R. Miliband and J. Saville).
20 For example, Ramsay MacDonald (as quoted in R. Miliband, *Parliamentary Socialism*, 2nd edn, Merlin Press, 1973, p. 20). MacDonald saw no 'profound gulf' between Liberalism and Socialism. And by 1903 he was anticipating the emergence of a 'united democratic party appealing to the people on behalf of a single, comprehensive belief in social reconstruction'.
21 The LRC changed its name in 1906 to the Labour Party.
22 For a good analysis of the impact of Marxism in Britain, see S. Pierson, *Marxism and the Origins of British Socialism*, Cornell University Press, 1973.
23 H. Pelling, *The Origins of the Labour Party 1880-1900*, Clarendon Press, Oxford, 1965, *passim*.
24 For a full account of the ILP and its history, see R. E. Dowse, *Left in the Centre*, Longmans, 1966.
25 Bruce Glasier, in *The Meaning of Socialism*, National Labour Press, 1919, provides a good illustration of this:
> Socialism, in truth, consists, when finally resolved, not in getting at all, but in giving; not in being served, but in serving; not in selfishness, but in unselfishness; not in the desire to gain a place of bliss in this world for one's self and one's family (that is the individualist and capitalist aim), but in the desire to create an earthly paradise for all . . . Yet it may be better simply to say with William Morris that Socialism is fellowship, and that fellowship is life, and the lack of fellowship is death. Fellowship is heaven and the lack of fellowship is hell.

(quoted in S. H. Beer, *Modern British Politics*, Faber & Faber, 2nd edn, 1969, p. 128.)
26 See T. Nairn, 'The Nature of the Labour Party', in Anderson, *op. cit.*
27 See R. Miliband, *op. cit.*, chs 1 and 2.
28 E.g. Robert Blatchford's *The Clarion*, 1892-1914.
29 It is, however, important to note that the 'ILP tradition' referred to here stems from the early years of the ILP—i.e. up to about 1920. During the 1920s and 1930s the ILP did indeed become a more socialist-oriented and theoretically sophisticated pressure group within the Labour Party (prior to its disaffiliation in 1932). But, by this time, it had lost its position of power and as it moved further Left so its chances of capturing the LP decreased. Moreover, the 'moral crusade' tradition of the early ILP has survived within the Labour Party, long after the ILP as an organization had moved to the Left.
30 See Webbs, *op. cit.*; Pelling, *op. cit.*; G. D. H. Cole, *British Working Class Politics 1832-1914*, Labour Book Service, 1941.
31 For reading on Fabianism, both its history and its ideology, see Bibliography.
32 Save to note that many of the most forceful and intelligent intellectuals of the age were involved with Fabianism, e.g. G. B. Shaw, the Webbs, G. D. H. Cole (later).
33 E.g., Beatrice Webb in *Our Partnership*, Longmans, 1948, p. 97, quoted in T. Nairn, *op. cit.* '[socialist society would be created and controlled by] an élite of unassuming experts . . . exercising the power inherent in superior knowledge and longer administrative experience.'
34 For an interesting discussion of the implications of a meritocratic system, see Michael Young, *The Rise of the Meritocracy*, Thames & Hudson, 1958 (Penguin Books, 1962).
35 J. M. Winter, *Socialism and the Challenge of War*, Routledge & Kegan Paul, 1974, p. 33. 'The Webbs' political thought is based on two central assumptions: first, that the consumption of necessary goods and services is the fundamental common interest of all men; and second, that government inevitably represented within given geographical boundaries "the interests of the citizen as a consumer".'
36 *Ibid.*, p. 51.
37 T. Nairn, *op. cit.*, p. 167.
38 See M. Cole, *The Story of Fabian Socialism*, Mercury Books, 1961.
39 The same might be said, on a grander scale, of the tiny Bolshevik group in Russia in the late-nineteenth and early-twentieth centuries.
40 The rapid centralization of national resources to cope with the War effort, see L. B. Seaman, *Post-Victorian Britain*, Methuen, 1966, ch. 9.
41 Trade Union membership (affiliated to TUC) figures: 1890 (estimated) 1·1 m; 1900 1·25 m; 1913 2·23 m; 1918 4·5 m; 1920 6·5 m (Source: S. H. Beer, *op. cit.*, p. 145).
42 For details see R. Miliband, *op. cit.*, ch 3.
43 Arthur Henderson, 1917, quoted in S. H. Beer, *op. cit.*, p. 149.
44 This was, of course, expressed within the Parliamentarist framework and was interwoven with an only semi-articulated acceptance of

Liberal ideology. The ILP was reformist through and through: just as Marx had characterized the creed of the capitalists as 'Accumulate, accumulate . . .', so the ILP motto might be 'Ameliorate, ameliorate . . .'. See R. E. Dowse, *op. cit.* and T. Nairn, *op. cit.*
45 See R. E. Dowse, *op. cit.* and G. Dangerfield, *op. cit.*
46 For a full discussion of the Labour Constitution and the way the Right has dominated, see R. T. McKenzie, *op. cit.*, Part 2, *passim.*
47 See R. T. McKenzie, *op. cit.*, chs 8 and 10.
48 The nationalization proposals of the 1945-51 government in fact conformed entirely to the public corporation blueprints originally suggested by Webb and the other Fabians. See R. Miliband, *op. cit.*, ch. 9.
49 Apart from the Communist Party, the ILP represented the only serious opposition: finding itself further and further removed from the central perspectives of the leadership, the ILP eventually disaffiliated from the Labour Party in 1932. Since then, it has led an increasingly pathetic existence as one of the least effective groups on the sectarian Left. There was considerable left-wing activity in the 1930s but this took place largely outside the Labour Party; and even those on the Left within the Party had little influence on the Party leadership.
50 The Houghton Committee's recommendations (1976) on Finances of Political Parties would, if implemented, have far-reaching implications for the Labour Party which would no longer be so heavily dependent financially upon the Trade Unions.
51 In the 1960s (from Frank Cousins to Hugh Scanlon) it seemed as though this alliance were likely to be broken as the Trade Union movement shifted to the left. However, the alliance has survived and indeed at the time of writing seems more firmly cemented than ever.
52 See R. Miliband, *op. cit.*, pp. 61-4 for details.
53 In particular the democratic control of industry, whilst couched in 'Socialist' terms, was in reality a Fabian proposal for centralized, public corporation ownership.
54 The two Labour governments of 1923-4 and 1929-31 were both minority administrations and there is thus some substance to the argument that neither had the chance to implement any socialist policies. Moreover, in 1929-31, the international slump presented special problems, to say the least.
55 See R. Miliband, *op. cit.* and D. Coates, *Labour and the Struggle for Socialism*, Cambridge University Press, 1974.
56 In the 1950s Gaitskell attempted his famous revision of Clause IV and tried to convert the Labour Party formally into a non-socialist party of liberal reform. On the theoretical level C. A. R. Crosland argued in *The Future of Socialism*, Cape, 1956, that society was now in a post-capitalist condition and 'traditional socialism' was therefore irrelevant.
57 I.e. in the first category—gas, electricity, airways; in the second—coal, rail transport.
58 For detailed expression of both 'Left' and 'Right' views, see R. Miliband, *op. cit.*, ch. 9; see also D. Coates, *op. cit.*, ch. 3.
59 For a good account of the historical development of the Welfare State see D. Fraser, *The Evolution of the British Welfare State*, Macmillan, 1973.

60 The major acts of 1945-51 in the Welfare field were: National Health Service Act 1946; National Insurance Act 1946; Education Act 1944; Family Allowance Act 1946; National Assistance Act 1948; Children Act 1948.
61 One of the major aims and functions of the early Trade Unions had been the provision of welfare services (see pp. 45-7).
62 Particularly France and Germany. For an excellent discussion of Marxism and democracy in Europe see G. Lichteim, *Marxism*, Routledge & Kegan Paul, 1961.
63 See pp. 44-50 and E. P. Thompson, *op. cit.*
64 As Miliband, *op. cit.*, points out, p. 372:
 the Labour Party is no longer even a 'reformist' party. 'Reformist' Socialism is the belief that a socialist society will be brought into being by way of a gradual series of structural and social reforms . . . . [This] is no longer the perspective which, however theoretically, informs the Labour leaders' approach to affairs.
65 See, particularly, C. A. R. Crosland, *op. cit.*, in which it is argued that we are now in a 'post-capitalist' situation where the 'old dogmas' are irrelevant. See also R. Jenkins's and C. A. R. Crosland's contributions to *New Fabian Essays*, ed. R. H. S. Crossman, Dent, 1952.
66 See T. Nairn, *op. cit.*
67 See N. Harris, *Competition and the Corporate Society*, Methuen, 1972, *passim*.
68 R. Miliband, *op. cit.*, p. 376.
69 See Bibliography.
70 Except Marcusians—and they, arguably, are not Marxists in any meaningful sense.
71 The definition of the ways in which Marxists see these tensions manifesting themselves forms an important part of the discussion in ch. 6.
72 Similarly, the questions arise with Western European Communist Parties (in France, Italy, Spain) as to why these parties have moved to the Right in recent years.
73 See, for example, R. T. McKenzie, *op. cit.*, chs 5 and 6.
74 Different, not least because the Left was by this time severely weakened within the Party (e.g., R. Miliband, *op. cit.*, ch. 10).
75 The NHS, largely Bevan's work, was created in 1946.
76 See D. Coates, *op. cit.*, pp. 190-7.
77 See *ibid.*, chapter 8, for a detailed expression of this view. For one of the most succinct and persuasive arguments of this position see the postscript to the second edition of R. Miliband's *Parliamentary Socialism*.
78 This forms one of the fundamental divisions between the two authors and is discussed at length in the final chapter.
79 E.g., A. B. Atkinson, *Economics of Inequality*, Oxford University Press, 1975; R. E. Dowse and J. Hughes, *Political Sociology*, Wiley, 1972; J. Kincaid, *Poverty and Equality in Britain*, Penguin Books, 1973; R. Blackburn, 'The Unequal Society', in J. Urry and J. Wakeford (eds), *Power in Britain*, Heinemann, 1973.

80 Although some Marxists, notably M. Barratt-Brown in *From Labourism to Socialism*, Spokesman Books, 1972, argue that the Welfare State has marked a significant shift, ideologically and specifically, towards Socialism. This argument is explored in more detail in ch. 6 in the context of the 'legitimation' question.
81 D. Coates, *op. cit.*, pp. 229-30.
82 Although R. Miliband has argued (*op. cit.*, postscript) that the Labour Party has ceased even to be fully reformist in its aims and performance. In the case of the majority of Labour leaders it is unlikely that any long-term perspective exists—nothing so theoretical as an idea can have passed through Mr Callaghan's head for many a year, if ever. But, as far as can be judged, the 'thinking people' in Labour's leadership—Owen, Dell, Shore, Williams, Healey and so on, maintain a perspective similar to that outlined.

Chapter five: Political directions in social work

1 *Case-Con*, 1977.
2 M. E. Richmond, *Social Diagnosis*, Russell Sage Foundation, 1917.
3 H. H. Perlman, *Casework: A Problem Solving Process*, University of Chicago Press, 1957.
4 F. Hollis, *Casework: A Psychological Therapy*, 2nd edn, Random House, 1972.
5 E.g., Z. Butrym, *The Nature of Social Work*, 1976, ch.4; and CCETSW Paper No. 10, *Education and Training for Social Work*, 1975.
6 J. Bronowski, *The Ascent of Man*, Bodley Head and BBC Publications, 1973.
7 R. Plant, *Social and Moral Theory in Casework*, Routledge & Kegan Paul, 1970, accepts the political aspects associated with practical values that contribute towards social work.
8 H. Lytton, 'Observation studies of parent-child interaction. A methodological review', *Child Development*, vol. 42, 1971, pp. 651-84; and M. Rutter, *Maternal Deprivation Reassessed*, Penguin Books, 1972, accept the unsatisfactory position in regard to adequate methodology in resolving complex questions such as parent-child interaction.
9 D. J. Pallis and B. E. Stoffelmyer, 'Social Attitudes and Treatment Orientation among Psychiatrists', *British Journal of Medical Psychology*, vol. 46, 1973, pp. 75-81, in relation to psychiatrists; C. Pritchard and A. W. J. Butler, 'Influence of Youth Tutor upon Teachers' Perception of some Maladjusted Behaviour', *Child Care, Health and Development*, vol. 1, 1975, pp. 251-61, in relation to school teachers; C. Pritchard and R. K. S. Taylor, *Variation in Perceptions within Professional Groups*, 1978, in relation to social workers—all have a tendency to respond on a personal level rather than an objective 'professional' level.
10 J. J. Spinetta and D. Rigler, 'The Child Abusing Parent. A Psychological Review', *Psychological Bulletin*, vol. 77, pt. 4, 1972, pp. 296-304.

11 S. M. Smith, *et al.*, 'Parents of Battered Babies: A controlled study', *British Medical Journal*, vol. 4, 1973, pp. 388-91.
12 I. Illich, *Medical Nemesis*, Calder & Boyars, 1975.
13 H. A. Prins, *Criminal Behaviour. An introduction to its study and treatment*, Pitman, 1973.
14 S. Cohen, 'It's all right for you to talk', in R. Bailey and M. Brake (eds), *Radical Social Work*, Arnold, 1975 (Cohen highlights some of the inconsistencies within traditional social work values yet recognizes that only a case specific approach, *attempting* not to be exploiting, judgmental, etc., is feasible for the radical and humane social worker).
15 See R. Holman, 'The Place of Fostering in Social Work', *British Journal of Social Work*, 5.1. 1975, pp. 3-29.
16 R. Greenberg, Paper to British Medical Association quoted in BASW News, *Social Work Today*, 3.10.1972, and DHSS, *Better Services for the Mentally Ill*, HMSO, 1973.
17 See C. Pritchard, 'The EWO, Truancy and School Phobia', *Social Work Today*, vol. 5, pt. 5, 1974, pp. 130-4; and Local Government Training Board (Ralphs Report) *Role and Training of the Education Welfare Officer*, HMSO, 1975. The research study showed that often the EWOs responded to complex cases with prosecution because of apparent lack of knowledge while the report highlighted the potential role as a social worker of the EWO and urged necessary training.
18 See R. M. Titmuss, *Social Policy*, George Allen & Unwin, 1974.
19 W. J. Patterson, *Social Work's Theory of Man*, Occasional Papers, New University of Ulster, 1976.
20 D. Sheppard, *Built as a City: God and the Urban World*, Hodder & Stoughton, 1974.
21 P. Freire, *Cultural Action for Freedom*, Penguin Books, 1972.
22 Despite the romantic aspect, Archbishop Lefebvre, 'A firm stand for Tradition', *Listener*, vol. 96, no. 2486, 1976, pp. 717-18, represents a still powerful voice in the Church.
23 P. Wedge and H. Prosser, *Born to Fail?*, Arrow Books, 1973; see also D. Bull (ed.), *Family Poverty*, Duckworth, 1971.
24 W. Jordan, *Poor Parents: Social Policy and the Cycle of Deprivation*, Routledge & Kegan Paul, 1974.
25 P. Leonard, 'Depression and Family Failure', *British Journal of Psychiatric Social Work*, 7.4.1964, pp. 191-7. While Leonard has virtually repudiated his earlier work, this paper still gives one of the best analyses of defensive apathy.
26 K. Horney, *New Ways in Psycho-Analysis*, Routledge & Kegan Paul, 1939.
27 The best known representatives of this 'school' are Hollis and Parad, see H. J. Parad, *Crisis Intervention*, FSAA, 1965, and H. J. Parad and R. R. Miller, *Ego-orientated Casework*, FSAA, 1971.
28 The client-centred approach of C. G. Rogers, *Client Centred Therapy*, Houghton Mifflin, 1951.
29 H. H. Perlman, *Casework in Social Work*, University of Newcastle Press, 1974, and T. L. Rapoport, *Social Casework: An appraisal and an affirmation*, Smith College Studies, 1974.
30 It appears to be increasingly recognized that such an approach offers

a humanizing service, and that to disregard the social casework orientation would be of some loss to clients facing the large bureaucracy. S. Cohen, *op. cit.*, and G. Pearson, 'Social Work as the Privatised Solution to Public Ills', *British Journal of Social Work*, 3.2.1973, pp. 209-28.
31 H. H. Perlman, *op. cit.*
32 *Case Con.*, 1977, is particularly vociferous in this direction—perhaps protesting too much?
33 S. Cohen, *op. cit.*, and G. Pearson, *op. cit.*
34 Examples are found in the legislation that 'created' social work, National Assistance Act 1948, National Health Service Act 1946, and to a lesser extent, Local Authority Social Service Act, 1970.
35 This would include not only all socialists, but also those within the conservative tradition, exemplified by Sir Keith Joseph.
36 S. Briar and H. Miller, *Problems and Issues in Social Casework*, Columbia University Press, 1971.
37 P. Leonard, 'Towards a Paradigm for Radical Practice', and M. Mayo, 'Community Development: A Radical Alternative?', in R. Bailey and M. Brake, *op. cit.*, 1975.
38 R. Lees, *Politics and Social Work*, Routledge & Kegan Paul, 1972.
39 R. Miliband, *Parliamentary Socialism*, 2nd edn, Merlin Press, 1973, p. 376.
40 S. Cohen, *op. cit.*
41 G. Pearson, *op. cit.*, 1975.
42 CCETSW, Paper No. 13, *Values in Social Work*, 1976; see also BASW booklet, *A Code of Ethics,* 1975.
43 For it has been argued that the establishment of social work is in itself something of a criticism of the society from which it evolved, see R. Plant, *op. cit.* See M. Rein: *Social Policy Issues of Choice and Change*, Random House, 1970.
44 E.g. R. Miliband, *The State in Capitalist Society*, Weidenfeld & Nicolson, 1969, chs 7 and 8.
45 G. Mungham, 'Social Workers and Political Action', in H. Jones (ed.), *Towards a New Social Work*, Routledge & Kegan Paul, 1975.
46 See, R. Bailey and M. Brake, *op. cit.*
47 R. M. Titmuss, *Commitment to Welfare*, Allen & Unwin, 1968.
48 S. Wiseman, *The Educational Obstacle Race*, Educ. Res. Fdn, 1973, Pallis and Stoffelmyer, *op. cit.*; Pritchard and Taylor, *op. cit.*
49 M. Mayo, *op. cit.* See D. Rice, cf. 'Microists and Macroists', *Social Work Today*, 6.16. 1975, pp. 512-16.
50 J. J. Spinetta and D. Rigler, 'The Child Abusing Parent: A Psychological Review', *Psychological Bulletin*, vol. 77, pt 4, 1972, pp. 296-304.
51 It is interesting to note that the concept of 'Clinical Freedom' in regard to doctors is not questioned but *explanations* of medicine are now being demanded and the rationality of decisions examined—social work need not feel too 'persecuted' when there are public demands for an explanation of social workers' actions.
52 CCETSW Paper No. 13, *op. cit.* See Olive Stevenson, Editorial, *British Journal of Social Work*, 3.4.1973, who made an impassioned

plea in defence of positive freedoms and protection against exploitation.
53 See E. Sainsbury, *Social Work with Families*, Routledge & Kegan Paul, 1975.
54 See C. Pritchard, 'An analysis of Parental Attitudes towards the Treatment of Maladjusted Children', *British Journal of Social Work*, 2.1.1972, pp. 69-81, where parents with problematic children were found to resist dealing with the problem until its 'seriousness' involved others outside the family. Also, D. Gath, *et al.*, *Child Guidance and Delinquency in a London Borough*. Oxford University Press, 1977, found a variation in demand for child psychiatric services apparently associated with parental response to the problem.
55 For example, M. Falsberg, 'Setting Limits with Juvenile Delinquents', *Social Casework*, March 1957, pp. 138-42, and R. Foren and R. Bailey, *Authority in Social Casework*, Pergamon Press, 1968.
56 A good example is the ideals behind the Mental Health Act, 1959, which R. M. Titmuss, *op. cit.*, called that most 'civilized Act' though its critics, e.g. L. A. Gostin, 'Human Condition', MIND, 1975, stress the *potential* abuses rather than accepting the need for control where and when appropriate, see K. Jones, 'The Wrong Target in Mental Health', *New Society*, vol. 39, no. 352, 1977, pp. 438-40.
57 See Butler Report, *Committee on the Mentally Abnormal Offender*, HMSO, Cmnd. No. 6244, 1975.
58 For example, P. Leonard, 'Explanation and Education in Social Work', *British Journal of Social Work*, 5.3.1975, pp. 325-34; M. McCormick, 'Social Advocacy: a New Dimension in Social Work', *Social Casework*, 3.11.1970.
59 For example, *Case-Con* on the one hand, the more polemical speeches of Sir Keith Joseph on the other.

Chapter six: The problems of legitimation

1 Such an argument is pursued by M. Barratt-Brown, *From Labourism to Socialism*, Spokesman Books, 1972.
2 B. Heraud, *Sociology of Social Work*, Pergamon Press, 1970.
3 Ralph Miliband, *The State in Capitalist Society*, Weidenfeld & Nicolson, 1969, p. 179.
4 E.g., R. Williams, *Communications*, Chatto & Windus, 1966.
5 As R. H. S. Crossman argued, *New Fabian Essays,* Dent, 1952.
6 E.g., R. T. McKenzie, *British Political Parties*, Mercury Books, 1959, *passim.*
7 B. Smith, *Policy Making in British Government*, Martin Robertson, 1976, *passim.*
8 E.g., R. A. Dahl, *A Preface to Democratic Theory*, University of Chicago Press, 1956.
9 Marxists would want to dispute that this is in fact the case: the cultivation of Labour bureaucracy and lack of working-class involvement has led the Labour Party to lose touch with its roots. See

B. Hindess, *Decline of Working Class Politics*, MacGibbon & Kee, 1971.
10 See ch. 4.
11 This section draws heavily on Ralph Miliband, *op. cit.*, chs 7 and 8.
12 In most West European countries this is the case although there are many exceptions—Spain and Greece, for example.
13 E.g., K. Marx and F. Engels, *The German Ideology*, Lawrence & Wishart, 1970 edn.
14 Described by Professor Gwyn Williams, as quoted in R. Miliband, *op. cit.*, p. 180 as 'an order in which a certain way of life and thought is dominant, in which one concept of reality is diffused throughout society in all its institutional and private manifestations, informing with its spirit all taste, morality, customs, religious and political principles, and all social relations, particularly in their intellectual and moral connotations'.
15 See British General Election studies published for each post-War election by Oxford University Press.
16 E.g., Jean Blondel, *Voters, Parties, Leaders*, Penguin Books, 1969 (rev. edn), pp. 91 and 98.
17 See R. Rose, *Influencing Voters*, 1967, quoted in R. Miliband, *op. cit.*, p. 188.
18 Although see pp. 31-5 for qualifications on this score: *vide* Mrs Thatcher succeeded Edward Heath.
19 R. Miliband, *Parliamentary Socialism*, 2nd edn, Merlin Press, 1973, p. 376.
20 R. Miliband, *The State in Capitalist Society*, p. 195.
21 This has been viciously analysed in Paul Foot, *The Politics of Harold Wilson*, Penguin Books, 1973.
22 I.e. H. Wilson, *The Labour Government, 1964-70*, Michael Joseph and Weidenfeld & Nicolson, 1971.
23 For the bizarre history of the modern Labour youth movement see P. Shipley, *Revolutionaries in Modern Britain*, Bodley Head, 1976, especially chs 4 and 5.
24 See chs 6 and 7.
25 R. Miliband, *The State in Capitalist Society*, p. 203.
26 For a provocative view of the political role of the police see Tony Bunyan, *History and Practice of the Political Police in Britain*, Friedman, 1976.
27 R. Miliband, *The State in Capitalist Society*, p. 216.
28 E.g., R. Miliband and J. Saville (eds), *Socialist Register*, 1973; Graham Murdoch and Peter Golding, *For a Political Economy of Mass Communications*, Merlin Press, 1973.
29 R. Miliband, *The State in Capitalist Society*, p. 242.
30 Barratt-Brown, *op. cit.*
31 R. Miliband, 'Marx and the State', *Socialist Register*, 1965, as quoted in Barratt-Brown, *op. cit.*, p. 69.
32 *Ibid.*, p. 70.
33 *Ibid.*, p. 90.
34 *Ibid.*, p. 95.
35 By Dorothy Thompson, for example, in an article in *New Reasoner*, no. 4, 1958, as quoted in *ibid.*, p. 77.

Chapter seven: Reform, revolution, or . . .?

1. R. M. Titmuss, *Essays on the Welfare State*, Routledge & Kegan Paul, 1957.
2. R. Pinker, *Social Theory and Social Policy*, Heinemann, 1971.
3. R. Dahrendorf, *The New Liberty*, Routledge & Kegan Paul, 1975.
4. There are many problems surrounding 'objectivity' of professional judgments: e.g., psychiatry, see L. A. Gostin, 'Human Conditions', *Mind*, vol. 1, 1975; also in 'general medicine', often considered to be based upon a 'hard' scientific approach, see I. Illich, *Medical Nemesis*, Calder & Boyars, 1975.
5. See M. Kidron, *Western Capitalism since the War*, Penguin edn, 1970. An interesting Marxist analysis of the 'permanent arms economy'.
6. A. Bevan, *In Place of Fear*, Heinemann, 1952, p. 169.
7. V. George and P. Wilding, *Ideology and Social Welfare*, Routledge & Kegan Paul, 1976.
8. C. A. R. Crosland, *The Future of Socialism*, Jonathan Cape, 1956.
9. This is not the place to elaborate the detailed economic analysis: but Ernest Mandel in his Introduction to *Das Kapital*, Penguin Marx Library, 1976, vol. 1, p. 23, has usefully listed Marx's predictions about the development of capitalism: 'the laws of accumulation of capital, stepped-up technological progress, accelerated increase in the productivity and intensity of labour, growing concentration and centralization of capital, transformation of the great majority of economically active people into sellers of labour-power, declining rate of profit, increased rate of surplus value, periodically recurrent recessions, inevitable class struggle between Capital and Labour, increasing revolutionary attempts to overthrow capitalism . . . .'
10. For example, the growth of ASTMS, NALGO, COHSE, APEX, etc., see R. Lumley, *White-collar Unionism in Britain*, Methuen, 1973.
11. Socialist brotherhood has not been much in evidence when one considers the record of schism, feud and purge in Communist Movements over the last fifty years.
12. See E. Crankshaw, *The Fall of the House of Habsburg*, Paladin, 1971, pp. 63-4. (Crankshaw, an avowed anti-Marxist, quotes Marx's letters to illustrate his prejudice against the 'lesser Central Europeans'.)
13. D. M. Thompson, *Europe Since Napoleon*, Penguin Books, 1957.
14. D. McClellan, *Marx*, Fontana, 1975, p. 70.
15. A. Marwick, *War and Social Change in the Twentieth Century*, Macmillan, 1974.
16. See Bibliography for 'New Left' writers.
17. E.g., the essays collected together in *Towards Socialism*, Fontana and New Left Books, 1965. For other reading in this area see Bibliography.
18. See M. Foot, *Aneurin Bevan, 1945-60*, Paladin edn, 1975, p. 18.
19. It may be thought that a hundred-year time span has little relevance to practising social workers, yet if the socio-political processes predicted by Marx have any validity, then a hundred years is a 'reasonable' period—consider how the 'pioneers' of the last century

would respond to today's freedoms, perhaps they would even be thought reactionary by present-day generations.
20 Quoted in R. Mishra, 'Marx and Welfare', *Sociological Review*, May 1975, pp. 287-313.
21 R. Mishra, *ibid*.
22 K. Marx, *Critique of the Gotha programme* (first published 1875).
23 Letter from Marx to Engels, as quoted in Mishra, *op. cit.* Also, noted by Engels in the Preface to *Das Kapital*, Lawrence and Wishart edn, vol. 1, p. 6.
24 R. Mishra, *op. cit.*
25 See A. Bullock, *Hitler: A Study in Tyranny*, Penguin Books, 1969 (associated with the Hitlerite racism of the 1930s was a frequent rationalization of political terror: assassination was justified because the victim was sexually deviant, e.g. Ernst Röhm).
26 It is, of course, a similar type of analysis that underlies the Trotskyist strategy of the 'transitional programme'.
27 R. Miliband, *Parliamentary Socialism*, 2nd edn, Merlin Press, 1973.
28 See, for example, article by R. Miliband in *Socialist Register*, 1976, ed. R. Miliband and J. Saville, Merlin Press, 1976.
29 See M. Foot, *op. cit.*
30 See Bibliography.
31 See K. Newton, *Sociology of British Communism*, Allen Lane the Penguin Press, 1969. The election figures from 1959 onwards were extrapolated from the *Guardian* final election results for the years 1964, 1966, 1970, 1974.
32 CCETSW Paper No. 13, *Values in Social Work*, 1976.
33 See M. Foot, *op. cit.*, p. 261 (Bevan's speech at the 1949 Blackpool Conference of the Labour Party).
34 Quoted in R. Mishra, *op. cit.*
35 See A. B. Atkinson, *The Economics of Inequality*, Oxford University Press, 1975; and J. Urry and J. Wakeford (eds), *Power in Britain*, Heinemann, 1973.
36 See J. Goldthorpe and D. Lockwood, *The Affluent Worker: industrial attitudes and behaviour*, Cambridge University Press, 1968; and by the same authors, *The Affluent Worker: political attitudes and behaviour*, Cambridge University Press, 1968; also, J. Westergaard and H. Resler, *Class in a Capitalist Society: a study of contemporary Britain*, Heinemann, 1975.
37 J. Hughes, 'Nationalisation and the Private Sector', in J. Urry and J. Wakeford, *op. cit.*
38 Marxists differ on the question of strategy of course. In the new draft of the Communist Party's *British Road to Socialism*, for example, the emphasis remains firmly upon cooperation with the existing Labour Party and an attempt at strengthening the 'Left-wing' within the Party.
39 P. Leonard in R. Bailey and M. Brake, *Radical Social Work*, Arnold, 1975.
40 Quoted in T. Bottomore, *Marxist Sociology*, Macmillan, 1976, p. 78.
41 Although it is important to note that Rosa Luxemburg was a fierce and consistent opponent of the Parliamentary, reformist road. Her

References to page 131

socialist democracy was firmly based in the revolutionary Marxian tradition.

42 K. Marx and F. Engels, *Manifesto of the Communist Party*, Foreign Language Press, Peking edn 1972 (first published 1848), p. 75.

Further reading

The following brief selection is suggested for additional reading in some of the areas of political study mentioned in the text:

Almond, G. and Verba, S. *The Civic Culture: Political Attitudes and Democracy in Five Nations*, Princeton University Press, 1963.
Anderson, P., *Considerations on Western Marxism*, New Left Books, 1977.
Barker, C., 'The British Labour Movement: aspects of current experience', in *International Socialism*, 61, pp. 40-8.
Blackburn, R., 'The New Capitalism', in *Towards Socialism*, Fontana and New Left Books, 1965.
Blackburn, R. (ed.), *Ideology and Social Science*, Fontana, 1972.
Blackburn, R. and Cockburn, A. (eds), *The Incompatibles: Trade Union Militancy and the Consensus*, Penguin Books, 1967.
Burke, E., *Thoughts on the Causes of the Present Discontents* (first published 1770), Oxford University Press, 1936.
Butler, D. and Stokes, D., *Political Change in Britain*, Macmillan, 1969.
Challinor, R., 'Labour and the Parliamentary Road', in *International Socialism*, 52, pp. 9-15.
Clegg, H., *et al.*, *A History of British Trade Unionism, vol. 1, 1889/1910*, Oxford University Press, 1964.
Foot, P., 'Parliamentary Socialism', in N. Harris and J. Palmer (eds), *World in Crisis*, Hutchinson, 1971.
Harris, N., *Beliefs in Modern Society*, Penguin Books, 1971.
Hyman, R., *Marxism and the Sociology of Trade Unionism*, Pluto Press, 1971.
Hyman, R., *Strikes*, Fontana, 1972.
Hyman, R. and Brough, I., *Social Values and Industrial Relations: a study of Fairness and Equality*, Blackwell, 1975.
Lane, T., *The Union Makes Us Strong*, Panther, 1975.
Lipset, S. M., *Political Man*, Mercury Books, London, 1963.
McBriar, A. M., *Fabian Socialism and English Politics 1884/1918*, Cambridge University Press, 1966.
Pritt, D. N., *The Labour Government 1945/51*, Lawrence & Wishart, 1963.

Further reading

Thompson, E. P., 'The Peculiarities of the English', in R. Miliband and J. Saville (eds), *Socialist Register*, Merline Press, 1965.
Widgery, D., *The Left in Britain 1956-68*, Penguin Books, 1976.
Williams, R. (ed.), *The May Day Manifesto*, Penguin Books, 1969.

Bibliography

Algie, J., *Social Values, Objectives and Action*, Kogan Page, 1974.
Allport, G. W., *The Nature of Prejudice*, Addison-Wesley, 1954.
Anderson, P. (ed.), *Towards Socialism*, Fontana and New Left Books, 1965.
Atkinson, A. B., *The Economics of Inequality*, Oxford University Press, 1975.
Avon, Lord, *The Eden Memoirs*, Cassell, 1960-5.
Bailey, R. and Brake, M. (eds), *Radical Social Work*, Arnold, 1975.
Baker, R., *Interpersonal Process in Generic Social Work*, Preston Institute of Technology Press, Victoria, Australia, 1976.
Barratt-Brown, M., *From Labourism to Socialism*, Spokesman Books, 1972.
Bartlett, H. M., *Common Base of Social Work Practice*, National Association of Social Workers, New York, 1970.
BASW, 'BASW to Make TV Programme', *Social Work Today*, 1977.
BASW, *A Code of Ethics for Social Workers*, 1975.
Beer, S. H., *Modern British Politics*, Faber & Faber, 2nd edn, 1969.
Bevan, A., *In Place of Fear*, Heinemann, 1952.
Biesteck, F., *The Casework Relationship*, Allen & Unwin, 1961.
Bitensky, R., 'Influence of Political Power in Determining The Theoretical Development of Social Work', *Journal of Social Policy*, 2.2., 1975, pp. 119-29.
Blackburn, R., 'The Unequal Society', in J. Urry and J. Wakeford (eds).
Blake, R., *The Conservative Party From Peel To Churchill*, Fontana, 1972.
Blatchford, R., *The Clarion*, 1892-1914.
Blondel, J., *Voters, Parties, Leaders* (rev. edn), Penguin Books, 1969.
Briar, S. and Miller, H., *Problems and Issues in Social Casework*, Columbia University Press, 1971.
Bronowski, J., *The Ascent of Man*, Bodley Head and BBC Publications, 1973.
Bull, D. (ed.), *Family Poverty*, Duckworth, 1971.
Bullock, A., *Hitler, A Study in Tyranny*, Penguin Books, 1969.
Bunyan, T., *History and Practice of the Political Police in Britain*, Friedman, 1976.

Bibliography

Burke, E., *Reflections on the Revolution in France*, Holst, 1965.
Butler, G., *The Tory Tradition*, Conservative Political Centre, 1957.
Butler, R. A., *The Art of the Possible*, Hamish Hamilton, 1971.
Butler Report, *Committee on the Mentally Abnormal Offender*, Cmnd 6244, HMSO, 1975.
Butrym, Z., *The Nature of Social Work*, Macmillan, 1976.
CCETSW, *Education and Training for Social Work*, Paper no. 10, 1975.
CCETSW, *Values in Social Work*, Paper no. 13, 1976.
Coates, D., *Labour and the Struggle for Socialism*, Cambridge University Press, 1974.
Cohen, S., 'It's All Right For You To Talk', in R. Bailey and M. Brake (eds).
Cole, G. D. H., *British Working Class Politics, 1832-1914*, Labour Book Service, 1941.
Cole, G. D. H. and Postgate, R., *The Common People*, 4th edn, Methuen, 1971.
Cole, M., *The Story of Fabian Socialism*, Mercury Books, 1961.
Crankshaw, E., *The Fall of the House of Habsburg*, Paladin, 1971.
Crick, B., *In Defence of Politics*, Penguin Books, 1962.
Crosland, C. A. R., *The Future of Socialism*, Jonathan Cape, 1956.
Crossman, R. H. S. (ed.), *New Fabian Essays*, Dent, 1952.
Dahl, R. A., *A Preface to Democratic Theory*, University of Chicago Press, 1956.
Dahrendorf, R., *The New Liberty*, Routledge & Kegan Paul, 1975.
Dangerfield, G., *The Strange Death of Liberal England*, MacGibbon & Kee, 1966.
DHSS, *Better Services for the Mentally Ill*, HMSO, 1973.
Dowse, R. E., *Left in the Centre*, Longmans, 1966.
Dowse, R. E. and Hughes, J., *Political Sociology*, Wiley, 1972.
Ennals, D., 'Six Contentious Months as Secretary of State', *Social Work Today*, 8.1.1977 and 'Hopes for 1977', *Social Work Today*, 8.12.1976.
Evans, R., 'Some Implications of an Integrated Model of Social Work for Theory and Practice', *British Journal of Social Work*, 6.2,1976, pp. 177-200.
Falsberg, M., 'Setting Limits with Juvenile Delinquents', *Social Casework*, March 1957, pp. 138-42.
Foot, M., *Aneurin Bevan, 1945-60*. Paladin, 1975.
Foot, P., *The Politics of Harold Wilson*, Penguin Books, 1973.
Foren, R. and Bailey, R., *Authority in Social Casework*, Pergamon Press, 1968.
Fowler, G., 'The Politics of Social Administration', unpub. paper, JUC AGM, 1977.
Fraser, D., *The Evolution of the British Welfare State*, Macmillan, 1973.
Freire, P., *Cultural Action for Freedom*, Penguin Books, 1972.
Fromm, E., *Fear of Freedom*, Routledge & Kegan Paul, 1969.
Galbraith, J. K., *The Age of Uncertainty*, André Deutsch, 1977.
Gath, D. *et al.*, *Child Guidance and Delinquency in a London Borough*, Oxford University Press, 1977.

Bibliography

George, V. and Wilding, P., *Ideology and Social Welfare*, Routledge & Kegan Paul, 1976.

Goldstein, H., *Social Work Practice—A Unitary Approach*, Columbia University Press, 1973.

Goldthorpe, J. and Lockwood, D., *The Affluent Worker: Political Attitudes and Behaviour*, Cambridge University Press, 1968.

Gostin, L. A. 'Human Condition', *Mind*, vol. 1, 1975.

Greenberg, R., paper to British Medical Association, BASW News, *Social Work Today*, 3.10,1972.

Harris, N., *Competition and The Corporate Society*, Methuen, 1972.

Heraud, B., *Sociology of Social Work*, Pergamon Press, 1970.

Hindess, B., *The Decline of Working Class Politics*, MacGibbon & Kee, 1971.

Hogg, Q., *The Case for Conservatism*, Penguin Books, 1947.

Hollis, F., *Casework: A Psychological Therapy*, 2nd edn, Random House, 1974.

Holman, R., 'The Role of Fostering in Social Work', *British Journal of Social Work*, 5.1.1972, pp. 3-29.

Holman, R., *Poverty*, Martin Robertson, 1977.

Horney, K., *New Ways in Psycho-Analysis*, Routledge & Kegan Paul, 1939.

Illich, I., *Medical Nemesis: The Expropriation of Health*, Calder & Boyars, 1975.

Jones, D. and Mayo, M., *Community Work: Two*, Routledge & Kegan Paul, 1975.

Jones, H. (ed.), *Towards a New Social Work*, Routledge & Kegan Paul, 1975.

Jones, K., 'The Wrong Target in Mental Health', *New Society*, vol. 39, no. 352, 1977, pp. 438-40.

Jordan, W., *Poor Parents: Social Policy and the Cycle of Deprivation*, Routledge & Kegan Paul, 1974.

Jordan, W., *Freedom and the Welfare State*, Routledge & Kegan Paul, 1976.

Kidron, M., *Western Capitalism Since the War*, Penguin Books, 1970.

Kincaid, J., *Poverty and Equality in Britain*, Penguin Books, 1973.

Koss, S., *Nonconformity in Modern British Politics*, Batsford, 1976.

Lees, R., *Politics and Social Work*, Routledge & Kegan Paul, 1972.

Lefebvre, Archbishop, 'A Firm Stand for Tradition', *Listener*, vol. 96, no. 2486, 1976, pp. 717-18.

Lenin, V. I., *Imperialism, The Highest Stage of Capitalism*, New York: International Publishers, 1939.

Leonard, P., 'Depression and Family Failure', *British Journal of Psychiatric Social Work*, 7.4.1964, pp. 191-94.

Leonard, P., 'Towards a Paradigm for Radical Practice', in Bailey and Brake (eds).

Leonard, P., 'Explanation & Education in Social Work', *British Journal of Social Work*, 5.3.1975, pp. 325-34.

Lichteim, G., *Marxism*, Routledge & Kegan Paul, 1961.

Lumley, R., *White-Collar Unionism in Britain*, Methuen, 1973.

Bibliography

Lytton, H., 'Observation studies of parent-child interaction. A methodological review', *Child Development*, 42, 1971, pp. 651-84.

McCormick, M., 'Social Advocacy and New Dimensions in Social Work', *Social Casework*, 3.11, 1970.

McKenzie, R. T., *British Political Parties*, Mercury Books, 1959.

McLellan, D., *Marx*, Fontana, 1975.

Mandel, E. (ed. with introduction) *Das Kapital. Vol. 1*, Penguin Marx Library, 1976.

Marwick, A., *War and Social Change in the Twentieth Century*, Macmillan, 1974.

Marx, K. and Engels, F., *The German Ideology*, Lawrence & Wishart, 1970.

Marx, K. and Engels, F., *Manifesto of the Communist Party*, Foreign Language Press, Peking, 1972.

Mayo, M., 'Community Development: A Radical Alternative?', in Brake and Bailey (eds).

Miliband, R., *The State in Capitalist Society*, Weidenfeld & Nicolson, 1969.

Miliband, R., *Parliamentary Socialism*, 2nd edn, Merlin Press, 1973.

Miliband, R. and Saville, J. (eds), *Socialist Register*, Merlin Press, annually from 1964.

Mishra, R., 'Marx and Welfare', *Sociological Review*, May 1975, pp. 287-313.

Mungham, G., 'Social Workers and Political Action', in Jones, H. (ed.).

Murdoch, G. and Golding, P., 'For a Political Economy of Mass Communications', in R. Miliband and J. Saville (eds), 1973.

Nairn, T., 'The Nature of the Labour Party', in Anderson, P. (ed.).

Newton, K., *Sociology of British Communism*, Allen Lane the Penguin Press, 1969.

Nichols, T. and Armstrong, P., *Workers Divided*, Fontana, 1976.

Oakeshott, M., 'On Being a Conservative', in *Rationalism in Politics*, Methuen, 1962.

Offer, D. and Offer, J. L., 'Growing Up: A Follow-up Study of Normal Adolescents', *Seminar Psychiatry*, 1.1.1969, pp. 46-56.

Pallis, D. J. and Stoffelmyer, B. E., 'Social Attitudes and Treatment Orientations among Psychiatrists', *British Journal of Medical Psychology*, 46, 1973, pp. 75-81.

Parad, H. J., *Crisis Intervention*, Family Service Association of America, 1965.

Parad, H. J. and Miller, R. R., *Ego-Orientated Casework*, Family Service Association of America, 1971.

Patterson, W. J., *Social Work's Theory of Man*, Occasional Papers, New University of Ulster, 1976.

Pearson, G., 'Social Work as the Privatised Solution to Public Ills', *British Journal of Social Work*, 3.2, 1973, pp. 209-28.

Pearson, G., 'The Politics of Uncertainty' in Jones (ed.)

Pearson, G., *The Deviant Imagination*, Macmillan, 1975.

Pelling, H., *History of Trade Unionism*, Macmillan, 1963.

Pelling, H., *The Origins of the Labour Party, 1880-1900*, Clarendon Press, 1965.

Bibliography

Perlman, H. H., *Casework. A Problem Solving Process*, University of Chicago Press, 1957.

Perlman, H. H., *Casework in Social Work*, University of Newcastle Press, 1976.

Pierson, S., *Marxism and the Origins of British Socialism*, Cornell University Press, 1973.

Pincus, A. and Minahan, A., *Social Work: Practice, Model and Method*, Peacock, 1973.

Pinker, R., *Social Theory and Social Policy*, Heinemann, 1971.

Plant, R., *Social and Moral Theory in Casework*, Routledge & Kegan Paul, 1970.

Prins, H. A., *Criminal Behaviour. An Introduction to its Study and Treatment*, Pitman, 1973.

Prins, H. A., 'Motivation for Social Work', *Social Work Today*, 5.2, 1974.

Pritchard, C., 'Analysis of Parental Attitudes Towards the Treatment of Maladjusted Children', *British Journal of Social Work*, 2.1, 1972, pp. 69-81.

Pritchard, C., 'The EWO, Truancy and School Phobia', *Social Work Today*, 5.5, 1974, pp. 130-4.

Pritchard, C. and Butler, A. W. J., 'Influence of Youth Tutor upon Teachers' Perception of some Maladjusted Behaviour', *Child Care, Health and Development*, vol. 1, 1975, pp. 251-61.

Pritchard, C. and Taylor, R. K. S., *Variation of Perception Within the Professional Group*, Leeds University (in press).

Radical Therapists, *Therapy Means Change not Adjustment*, Penguin Books, 1975.

Ralphs Report, *Role and Training of the Education Welfare Officer*, Local Government Training Board, HMSO, 1975.

Rapaport, T. L., *Social Casework. An Appraisal and An Affirmation*, Smith College Studies, 1974.

Rein, M., *Social Policy: Issues of Choice and Change*, Random House, 1970.

Rice, D., 'Microists & Macroists', *Social Work Today*, 6.16, 1975, pp. 512-16.

Richmond, M. E., *Social Diagnosis*, Russell Sage Foundation, 1917.

Roberts, R. and Nee, R., *Theories of Social Casework*, University of Chicago Press, 1970.

Rogers, C. G., *Client-Centred Therapy*, Houghton-Mifflin, 1951.

Rutter, M., *Maternal Deprivation Reassessed*, Penguin Books, 1972.

Sainsbury, E., *Social Work with Families*, Routledge & Kegan Paul, 1975.

Seaman, L. B., *Post-Victorian Britain*, Methuen, 1966.

Seed, P., *The Expansion of Social Work in Britain*, Routledge & Kegan Paul, 1973.

Sheppard, D., *Built as a City: God and the Urban World*, Hodder & Stoughton, 1974.

Shipley, P., *Revolutionaries in Modern Britain,* Bodley Head, 1976.

Smith, B., *Policy Making in British Government*, Martin Robertson, 1976.

Bibliography

Smith, S. M. *et al.*, 'Parents of Battered Babies, A Controlled Study', *British Medical Journal*, vol. 4, 1973, pp. 388-91.

Solzhenitsyn, A., *Warning to the Western World*, Bodley Head and BBC Publications, 1976.

Spinnetta, J. J. and Rigler, D., 'The Child Abusing Parent: A Psychological Review', *Psychological Bulletin*, vol. 77, pt 4, 1972, pp. 296-304.

Stevenson, O., Editorial, *British Journal of Social Work*, 3.4.1973.

Tawney, R. H., *Religion and the Rise of Capitalism*, Penguin Books, 1964.

Thompson, D., 'Welfare State', *New Reasoner Journal*, vol. 4, 1958.

Thompson, D., *Nonconformity in the Nineteenth Century*, Routledge & Kegan Paul, 1972.

Thompson, D. M., *Europe Since Napoleon*, Penguin Books, 1957.

Thompson, E. P., 'Open Letter to Lesek Kolakowski', in R. Miliband and J. Saville (eds), 1973.

Thompson, J. A., *The Collapse of the British Liberal Party*, Heath, 1961.

Timms, Noel, *Social Casework*, Routledge & Kegan Paul, 1964.

Timms, Noel, 'Child Guidance—A Pilot Survey', in MacLachlan, *Problems and Progress in Medical Care*, Routledge & Kegan Paul, 1968.

Titmuss, R. M., *Essays on the Welfare State*, Routledge & Kegan Paul, 1957.

Titmuss, R. M., *Commitment to Welfare*, Allen & Unwin, 1968.

Titmuss, R. M., *Social Policy*, Allen & Unwin, 1974.

Townsend, P. (ed.), *The Concept of Poverty*, Heinemann, 1970.

Urry, J. and Wakeford, J. (eds), *Power in Britain*, Heinemann, 1973.

Vincent, J., *The Formation of the British Liberal Party 1857-68*, Constable, 1966.

Webb, S. and B., *History of Trade Unionism*, 2nd edn, Longmans, 1920.

Wedderburn, D., 'Facts and Theories of the Welfare State', in Miliband and Saville (eds), 1965).

Wedderburn, K. W., *The Worker and the Law*, Penguin Books, 1965.

Wedge, P. and Prosser, H., *Born to Fail?*, Arrow Books, 1973.

Westergaard, J. and Resler, H., *Class in a Capitalist Society: a Study of Contemporary Britain*, Heinemann, 1975.

Williams, R., *Communications*, Chatto & Windus, 1966.

Williams, R., *Keywords*, Fontana, 1976.

Wilson, H., *The Labour Government, 1964-70*, Michael Joseph and Weidenfeld & Nicolson, 1971.

Wilson, T., *The Downfall of the Liberal Party, 1914-35*, Fontana, 1968.

Winter, J. M., *Socialism and the Challenge of War*, Routledge & Kegan Paul, 1974.

Wiseman, S., *The Educational Obstacle Race*, Educational Research Foundation, 1973.

Woodroofe, K., *From Charity to Social Work*, Routledge & Kegan Paul, 1962.

Young, M., *The Rise of the Meritocracy*, Penguin Books, 1962.

Young, P., *Foreword: Values in Social Work*, CCETSW Paper no. 13, 1976.

Index

Allende, S., 66, 122
Allport, G. W., 26
America: and populism, 94; social work in, 77
Armed Forces, 101-2
authoritarianism, 107-8

baby battering, 69-70, 82
Baker, R., 9
Baldwin, S., 30, 122
Barratt-Brown, M., 106 f
BASW, 13
Beer, S., 22, 33
Benn, A., 63
Bentham, J., 42 f
Bevan, A., 63, 112, 121, 124-6
Biesteck, F., 28
Blake, R., 25
Boyle, Lord, 33
Brown, G., 19
bureaucracy, 47, 72 f, 126-9
Burke, E., 23
Butler, R., 28, 33, 104

capitalism: and legitimation, chapter 6 *passim*; and social democracy, chapter 4 *passim*
Catholicism, 19
CCETSW, 14, 79
Chamberlain, N., 58
change, 79-83, 110-11
Chartism, 45
Children Act: (1948), 10; (1975), 84
Children and Young Persons Act: (1969), 10; (1963), 84

Client: response of, 80, 83; self-referral, 71
CND, 55, 63
Coates, D., 66
Cohen, S., 77-8
collectivism, 51 f, 75
comfort/amelioration, 83
common ownership, 73 f, 126
Communism/Communists, 19, 20, 112, 115, 118, 119, 131
Communist Parties, 61, 91, 122
community action, 55, 63
community work, 97, 128
conflict, 1, 79 f, 85 f
consensus, 1, 23-4, 129-31
Conservatism, chapter 3 *passim*; and capitalism, 110-11; in crisis, 31-3, 38-9; and the Labour Movement, 31-3; and the landed interest, 22 f; and imperialism, 26-7 f; and individualism, 28 f; and 'Old Tory' ideas, 20-5; psychological attraction of, 22-3; and religion, 20-1, 26; and social welfare, 21-2, 33-5; and social work, 72-5, 80; and the State, 27-35, 37-8; and Tory democracy, 25-7, 33
control, 10, 13, 51-3, 76, 83-5
Corn Laws, Repeal of, 25
Crick, B., 1
Crosland, C. A. R., 19, 59, 113

democratic socialism, 5-6, 112-13, chapter 7 *passim*; and Aneurin Bevan, 63, 112-13; and the ILP tradition, 48-50

159

Index

Disraeli, B., 22, 24 f, 28, 33
dual dilemma, 6, 14, 71 f, 76-7, 79

Education Act (1944), 10, 84, 104
education system, 20, 103-4
EEC, 30, 32
embourgeoisement, 126
Engels, F., 131
Ennals, D., 8

Fabianism *see* Labour Party
false consciousness, 62
Fascism, 112
Fascists, 20
Foot, M., 117
Free Trade, 42
Freire, P., 73
Freudians, 2, 72-6, 119

Gaitskell, H., 59, 113
Gath, D., 11
Green, T. H., 43

Hailsham, Lord (formerly Quintin Hogg), 20, 28
Hardie, K., 66
Harris, N., 29 f, 35-9
Henderson, A., 54
Heraud, B., 90
heresy response, 15-16
Horney, K., 76

Illich, I., 70, 73
imperialism, 26-7
Incomes Policy, 121
Independent Labour Party (ILP) *see* Labour Party
individualism, 1-2, 10-14, 27-8, 72-6, 81-2

Jenkins, R., 102
Jordan, W., 10, 13, 28
Joseph, Sir Keith, 8, 31, 33, 75, 80

Labour Party, chapter 4 *passim*; and bureaucracy, 47, 50 f, 126-7; and Fabianism, 50 f, 99; and the ILP, 48-50; 96; and the Parliamentarist tradition, 47 f, 65-7; and socialism, chapter 7 *passim*; and the State, 53-67, 99 f; and the Trade Unions, 45-50
Labour Representation Committee (LRC), 45, 50

Lansbury, G., 66
Lees, R., 1, 77
legitimation, chapter 6 *passim*, 3-6, 56 f, 62 f, 121
Lenin, V. I., 26, 96, 117, 124-7
Leonard, P., 10, 80
Liberalism, chapter 4 *passim* (especially pp. 40-5), 12 f
Lloyd George, 54, 58
Luxemburg, R., 131

MacDonald, J. R., 67, 99
Macmillan, H., 22, 33
Maxton, J., 66
Marxism/Marxist, chapter 7 *passim*, 5, 10, 77-9, 85-7; analysis of conservatism, 35-9; and the contradictions of capitalism, 37-8, 105-9, 113-14, 125 f; criticisms of, 113 f; and evolutionary change, 105-9, 117 f; and the Labour Party, 49-50, 99-101; and social democracy, 61-7, 90 f; and social work, 4-5, 85-7, 96-7, 108-9; and the Welfare State, 64-5, 118-19
media, 20, 102-3
Mental Health Act (1959), 84
mental illness, 84
Miliband, R., 56, 61, 67, 91, 97, 99, 101, 104, 108
Mill, J. S., 43
Mishra, R., 118
monarchy, 26-7
moral-ethical, 1-2, 72-4, 77-8
motivation, 14 f
Murdoch, G. and Golding, P., 103

Nairn, T., 52
National Front, 122-3
National Assistance Act (1948), 84
National Enterprises Board (NEB), 58
National Health Service Act (1946), 84
Nationalization *see* common ownership
Nazis, 20
New Left, 116, 122, 128
New Model Unions *see* Trade Unions
New Unions *see* Trade Unions
Nonconformism, 44, 47-50, 101
nuclear war, dangers of, 105-6, 111, 127

Orwell, G., 85, 111
Owen, R., 45

Index

parliamentary democracy, 92-7
Pearson, G., 10, 77, 79
Peel, R., 24-5
perceptions, clash of, 14-16, 69-70, 80-1
Perlman, H., 68, 76
Pinker, R., 110
Plant, R., 12
pluralism, 90 f
police, 101-2
political culture, chapters 3 and 4 and 6 *passim*, 3-5, 78, 120
Poor Law, 43
poverty, 11, 121, 124-5
Powell, E., 30
pressure-groups, 4, 93
probation service, 84
professionalism, 111
psychiatric 'deluge', 11
psycho-analytical, 74
psycho-pathological, 1-2, 72, 74-6
psycho-social, 1, 3-4, 72, 76-7
public ownership *see* common ownership
public schools, 104

racial prejudice, 26-7, 116, 119
radical-political, 1, 4-6, 77-8, 82-3, 85-7
radical therapists, 11
rationality argument, 23-4, 49 f
Ralph's Report (1974), 71-2
reform, 3-4, 10-14, 76-83
reformism, chapter 4 *passim*, chapter 7 *passim*
revolution, chapter 4 (especially pp. 61-7); chapter 7 *passim*
Richmond, M., 28
Rogers, C., 76
Rousseau, J.-J., 43

Shaw, G. B., 8, 15, 124
Sheppard, D. (Bishop of Liverpool), 73
Smith, B., 8
social administration, 8-9, 69-70
social contract, 100-1
social democracy, 3-6, 71, 85-7, chapter 4 *passim*; and the legitimation debate, 90-7
Social Democratic Federation (SDF), 48
socialism, chapter 7 *passim*; and the Labour Party and Labour Movement, chapter 4 *passim*

socio-economic deprivation, 74-7
social policy, 8-9, 72 f
social service departments, 9, 80, 82
social sciences: limitations in relation to social work, 69-70
social work: aims of, 78-87; American, 77; development of, 3, 9-10; methods of, 1-3, 12 f, 68 f, 71-9; political role, chapters 1, 4 and 7 *passim*; practice, 78 f, 82-3; profession, 3, 68 f; range of intervention, 7-10, 68 f; statutory powers, 84-5; values, 12-14, 136, chapters 6 and 7 *passim*
social worker: authority, 83-5; background, 71; ideological assumptions, 15-16, 72-9, 82-3, 85-7, 110; multi-method, 9
Solzhenitsyn, A., 7
Stalin, J., 122, 128-9
State, the, 14, 27-33, 35-9; and social democracy, chapter 4 *passim*; and theories of legitimation, chapter 6 *passim*; and socialist politics, chapter 7 *passim*
stigmatization, 10
systems theory, 9

Timms, N., 7, 11
Titmuss, R., 80, 110
Thatcher, M., 28, 31-3, 35, 38-9
Trade Unions, chapter 4 *passim* (especially pp. 45-50); and ideology, 45-8; and legislation, 26, 46-7; and legitimation, chapter 6 *passim*; and Liberalism, 44-8; New Model, 45 f; New Unions, 48 f; and politics *see* Labour Party; and Revolution, 49-50; and 'white-collar' workers, 107, 113
Tredinick, A., 14
'Tribune' Group, 50, 66
Trotsky, L., 117

uncertainty (of social work role), 7, 11-12, 15
unitary approach, 9
Utilitarianism, 41 f, 51

value systems (in social work), 7, 12-16, 70, 72-9, 87
violence, 105-6, 111, 127-8

Webb, B. and S., 47, 52, 56
Wedge, P. and Prosser, H., 75

Index

welfare: as a socialist principle, 106-9, 118
welfare rights, 68
Welfare State, 3-5, 17, 21-2, 33-5, 57-9, 63-5, 76-7, 105-9
'white-collar' TU, *see* Trade Unions
Wilson, Sir Harold, 58, 99, 102, 122
Winter, J. M., 52
workers' control, 54-8, 128-9

working class, 42, 131; and the ILP, 48-50; and Fabianism, 51-61; and false consciousness, 62
Woodroofe, K., 11
Workers' Revolutionary Party (WRP), 102

Young, G., 85